EVER-WIDENING CIRCLES

CIRCLES

OR

ROAD TO BABA

A Memoir

BRENDA HANCOCK

"All that you have learned and experienced in life is meaning-
less, until you can say *"Aham Brahmasmi"* (I am Brahman).
Then, all your attachments fall away and you become fearless."

Baba in Silence, in conversation, (speaking with his hands).

Therefore, this memoir is offered in deep humility.

PAGE PUBLISHING, INC.
New York, NY

First originally published by Page Publishing, Inc. 2016

ISBN 978-1-68409-962-7 (Paperback)
ISBN 978-1-68348-476-9 (Hard Cover)
ISBN 978-1-68348-475-2 (Digital)

Printed in the United States of America

CONTENTS

PART I:
BEFORE

PART II:
AFTER

PART I: BEFORE

Chapter One

A Glimpse of the Future

"I know Everything," wrote Baba, with a particularly beautiful smile—and I did not doubt it. In fact, I was finding it very reassuring to be with someone who clearly knew me and everything about me better than I knew myself. If you know nothing is hidden, what is there to worry about?

We were in Baba's home in Simla, now called Shimla, in the foothills of the Himalayas; it was 1972. I had taken a career break after four years teaching in Kenya and ten as the head of a newly founded international school for girls in southern England. Like many others, I had come to India in the hope of finding something, or someone, special. By nature a believer, though not of the church-going kind, I had read a lot, listened a lot, gone from time to time to London to see and hear currently popular spiritual personalities, attended meetings, talks, courses, and meditation groups—always searching for something that would seem, to me, one hundred percent real. Now the search was over; I had found—or been found by—the One I was looking for. It had taken forty years.

Back to the Beginning...

This time it all started for me in 1932 when I was born to British parents in Tsingtao, a coastal town of northern China. Until I was seven, we lived in various places along the coast of China where my father was employed by the pre-communist Chinese government as an officer of the Maritime Customs, an administrative service that employed a number of foreigners. A proud claim later, during my early school days in England, was that my father spoke, read, and wrote Mandarin Chinese; it must have meant little or nothing to the hearers. I have always been pleased that China was the land of my birth.

Probably most people's early childhood memories have blank interludes, like a film going in and out of focus. My earliest memory is of my father who seemed immensely tall to my infant eyes as I lay in my cot; in fact, he was six foot four. The next memory I have is of being in England with father and mother, my older brother and a White Russian woman from the Ukraine who was employed to help look after us. This was in 1935. Father was entitled to a year's home leave every five years. We must have undertaken the long journey to England by sea, but I have no memory of that.

We were staying in a small hotel near the home of our grand-parents who lived in Kempsey, a small town in Worcestershire in the west of England. We spent most of the days with them and Father's youngest sister, our Aunt Olive. Grandfather Hancock, a gracious and thoughtful man who had somehow survived the 1914–1918 war as a colonel in the British army and had been decorated for his valor, was now struggling to make a living by running a chicken farm. I remember accompanying him as he laboriously wheeled tubs full of water to the outlying parts of his smallholding. It was fun for me as I chattered along by his side but must have been hard and backbreaking work for him.

Grandmother was equally hard-working. The house was kept spotless; excellent home baking went on in the kitchen. All the bed linen was crisp and white—no washing machines then, just a boiler, a bar of soap, a scrubbing board, and sheer hard labor. There was a small beautifully kept flower garden and an enormous fluffy gray cat named Bun.

It was a daily task for the grown-ups to sit round the kitchen table cleaning one by one the eggs laid by grandfather's hens, an activity I would watch though no one asked me to help. It seems that I did sometimes try to be useful around the house since one day I was laboriously climbing the stairs, carrying a large broom and a dustpan, when my aunt asked me where I thought I was going. At this, I am told, I turned round and grandly informed her, "Me go upstairs. By 'n' by, me come down again". So there! Much amused by this unconscious put-down, my aunt would often remind me of it.

Later that year, the family visited Norway. For part of the time we stayed in a hotel in Lillehammer; by now it was winter for I can still see in my mind's eye the brightly colored houses standing out against the white snow. One day my brother Leslie, Olga our Russian carer, and I went tobogganing on a slope near the hotel. Leslie had one toboggan and Olga and I shared another. After a glorious if bumpy ride down the hill, we two landed unceremoniously in a snow-filled ditch by the side of the road and—no doubt this is what imprinted the incident on my memory—I ended up in the ditch with our substantial Russian friend on top of me. Meanwhile, Leslie, a big boy of the great age of six, was trudging up and skidding bumpily down the slope on his own and reveling in it. I heard it said that I was the fattest child in that hotel—hardly a flattering distinction but not particularly wounding to the spirit when one is three years old.

Early in the following year, by which time we were back in England, Father left us to return to China since his leave was coming to an end. In those days the sea journeys took about a month. There is then another substantial lapse of memory, and several months later, we too were arriving back in China, this time in the northern coastal port of Wei Hai Wei. Father came on board to greet us. This was an exciting reunion, eagerly anticipated by all of us, but I remember staring at my father with blank astonishment when the great moment came and exclaiming, "Daddy, you've *shrunk!*" This remark only added to the general merriment of the occasion but I was genuinely baffled. It took me years to work out that my angle of vision had changed since I had last seen Father.

Wei Hai Wei, 1936

In Wei Hai Wei, our Russian friend who had a husband and home in Shanghai was replaced by an Englishwoman named Kit Phillips— Miss Phillips to us. She was about the same age as my mother and they became good friends. She taught us children our letters and numbers, creating a cheerful attitude to learning, which probably stood us in good stead later when we went to school. She and our mother would accompany us on outings, to the beach in summer when we swam in the sea and ice-skating in winter when even the sea froze over. Miss Phillips made and left with us a photographic record of our home and family and of colorful local rituals and ceremonies, some of which are, no doubt, by now long relegated to a superstitious past.

One of my delights in Wei Hai Wei was to be taken for a walk up the hill behind our home where an unknown artist had carved into some rocks with exquisite detail a miniature world of people and houses, streets, pagodas, and little bridges. To me it was a wonderland, and I could never have enough of it. Another, very different, treat was to be taken on board vessels of the British Navy, which used to visit Wei Hai Wei from time to time. We privileged expatriate children were received with great kindness by the captains and crews, shown all over the ships and given refreshments. Before we left to return to shore, each of us would be given as a memento a black ribbon hatband with the ship's name embroidered on it in gold thread. I still have hatbands from *HMS Hermes* and *HMS Grimsby*, both of which were lost during World War II.

In Wei Hai Wei, my father had the rank of acting Commissioner of Chinese Customs. This meant that we lived in a pleasant single-storied house on a hill overlooking the bay, with a large and well-stocked garden. As children we were much impressed by the fact that whenever our father used his official launch, he was entitled to fly a flag announcing his presence. On one occasion, he took us in the launch—flag flying, of course—across the bay to Wei Hai Wei Island where we were to attend a party given by another expatriate family. I was wearing a new blue party frock, which I thought very pretty. I made the mistake of confiding this to my father who did not approve of little girls making admiring comments about their own appearance and said so, firmly. That was my first lesson in conventional modesty.

All too soon, Father was posted to Shanghai, so once again the family was on the move and everything had to be packed up into boxes and trunks. The lovely Wei Hai Wei days were over.

Pre-War Shanghai

In Shanghai we had a modest three-storied house with a small garden, in what was then called Sinza Road—number 1665, to be precise. Mother's parents were long-established residents of Shanghai and had a beautiful family home, which was where, after some rather perfunctory education in a small boarding school in southern England (they took some examinations but never knew whether they had passed since no one cared to find out), Mother and her twin sister,

Lesley, grew to adulthood with their elder brother and two younger sisters. My parents employed a Chinese driver for their Austin Seven car, a cook and a house servant, and here we children were once again looked after for the most part by Olga. Miss Phillips took a teaching post in Shanghai at the Cathedral School for Girls and was later interned by the Japanese until the end of the approaching world war.

Despite all the great indignities suffered by Chinese people over the years at the hands of foreigners, the Chinese employed by my parents were extraordinarily loyal to the family and kind and protective of us children. Even after my mother, brother and I had left for England in 1939 and become stranded there owing to the outbreak of the European war, they sent gifts for us with my father when he came to England in 1940 to enlist in the Royal Air Force. I still treasure mine: a small carved wooden buffalo and rider set on a carved ebony stand, and a set of three books, in English, but put together in the old Chinese way with carved wooden covers and pages that open concertina-fashion from the back. To accompany each page of text, there are illustrations hand-painted on silk. The three books tell the stories of rice, tea, and silk.

That of course came later. Now in Shanghai life followed a slightly different pattern, for we were living in a very big city, one of the largest in the world as I was told at the time. There were foreign 'concessions' along the coast and large expatriate communities, the men mainly engaged in business. My mother's father, William Seaton King, born in China, was in the tea trade and other businesses in East Asia all his working life. The European adults had a thriving social life with their dinners and cocktail parties; we children had our own parties, usually requiring fancy dress. My brother used to go as a pirate with a red bandanna round his head and a luxuriant painted moustache; I was always dressed up as the Knave of Hearts in a special costume made by our talented Russian carer.

We still lived mainly a nursery life until we went to school, though there was also a small garden to play in. Next door to us was a girl called Elizabeth Joan, six months older than me, with whom I often played. In our Shanghai days, Elizabeth Joan, my brother and I would be taken on outings to nearby Jessfield Park where there were a large pond and, to our eyes, very big carved stone Chinese lions. Being by those few months my senior, EJ went to school first and could share with me some of the things she had been learning. I have an enjoyable memory of a very muddled version of the old childhood game of "quis?" and 'ego' solemnly imparted by her as we two squatted by the side of the pond.[1] "Take a daisy, like this" she said, "the yellow part in the middle is the egg, and you take off these pink-and-white petals one by one, and they are the answers." Or perhaps they were the bacon? Anyway, I was sufficiently impressed by this evidence of the wonders of going to the big school and learning things to remember the incident all my life.

Occasionally too, there would be an outing with our mother to a big department store called Wing On's, via a bustling street known as Bubbling Well Road. Every street in the city was thronged with Chinese pedestrians, who spilled over from the sidewalks onto the thoroughfare so that our driver had to go very slowly to avoid an accident.

There were, in the middle and late 1930s, millions of refugees from the Japanese invasion of Manchuria and the political fighting in the north, many of whom camped in desperate conditions just outside Shanghai, and the city itself was extremely crowded. As a child, I was deeply affected by the sight of the beggars in the streets; one, in particular, I have never forgotten, a man with four visible

---

1. This was a vestige of the old classics-centered education: a child who had something to give would shout "quis?" (who?) and the first to answer "ego!" ('I' in Latin and nothing whatever to do with eggs) would need to be ready to catch whatever was on offer.

stumps where his limbs had been, who was left to lie in the street in dirty white rags to beg. As we walked by on that occasion, I badly wanted to give something but was hurried on. So many times, Olga said, limbs were tied back to look as though they were missing—true or not, there was no possibility of fraud in the case of that man. After my childhood experiences in Shanghai, limited though they were and sheltered as I was, I always felt that I understood what people meant when they talked about suffering humanity. Long before television brought images of fearful suffering into people's homes all over the world, I had seen it at close range.

Formal schooling for me, as a foreigner, began in a very junior class at the above-mentioned Cathedral School for Girls, the first of six schools I eventually attended. I was permanently overawed there and my reports, carefully kept by my mother till the end of her life, all reiterated the need for more confidence. I doubt if I learned much, but the school had a good reputation. My brother, of course, went to an equivalent Cathedral School for Boys.

Father was a tall man. At work in Wei Hai Wei, 1936.

Winter in Wei Hai Wei, "when even the sea froze over."

Mother in the garden
in Shanghai, 1938.

Fancy dress.

Tsingtao, 1937

The summer in Shanghai is uncomfortably hot and humid. Father had to stay and sweat it out, literally, for there was no air-conditioning. My mother, brother, and I, together with Olga, went at least once to Tsingtao (now Xingdao) during those months of the year. There was one summer when we were staying there in a small rented house. That was in 1937, the year when Shanghai was bombed and full-scale war between Japan and China began. As already mentioned, there had been hostilities in the north long before and, while we were staying in Tsingtao, there were often Japanese soldiers to be seen, possibly on leave, but Japan had not yet declared war on foreigners. Mother carefully impressed on us the need to fall off our bicycles towards the ditch and not the road if we were frightened by a Japanese armored vehicle roaring up behind us, which was something some of the young soldiers were known to do as a prank. She had a suitcase ready and fully packed all the time, in case we should need to leave precipitately.

Tsingtao had a long, wide sandy beach with a mound of large boulders at the far end. One treat we enjoyed was to be taken for rides on the donkeys standing with their Chinese owners at the entrance to the beach, waiting for custom. I always longed to be allowed to choose the shabbiest donkey with the poorest-looking owner since I was sure they needed our money the most; but again, Olga thought differently, and we were firmly led to the smartest donkeys with the most prosperous-looking owners. Probably she was motivated by considerations of safety or hygiene but I would not have thought of that.

One day something unusual and exciting happened. As we ambled along on our donkeys about twenty yards from the water's edge with the donkey owners accompanying us on foot, two young Japanese soldiers who were paddling in the shallows decided to have some fun with us. One chose my brother's donkey, which was ahead of mine, and the other chose mine. Laughing and shouting to each other, they ran swiftly up the beach and tried to jump over the heads of our donkeys, which, despite the restraining efforts of their owners, bolted leaving the owners far behind. Leslie was very happy with the sudden gallop, but I was desperately clinging onto my donkey's saddle, lost my footing from one of the stirrups and felt myself to be in great danger of falling off as we were approaching the boulders at the far end of the beach. I did not know the donkeys would stop there since there was nothing much else they could do, so for a few moments, I was really frightened. Once the donkeys came to a halt, I got my balance back and confidence returned—then, heartless children that we were, we could both enjoy the spectacle of Olga gesticulating wildly in the distance, terribly anxious about her charges and doing her best to run on the soft sand in our direction. And *how* she scolded those two donkey owners; she even refused them all payment, which was very unfair since what had happened was not their fault at all.

We never did have to leave Tsingtao suddenly, despite our mother's precautions, nor did we ever have occasion to make sure we fell off our bicycles into a ditch. However, the circumstances and the general situation were such that Father did not want us to return at once to Shanghai at the end of our stay but wanted us to go instead to Singapore. We took a boat from Tsingtao to Nagasaki where Mother contrived to find us berths on a ship that was setting sail for Singapore.

Singapore, 1937–'8

In Singapore, we stayed at first for several weeks at the Goodwood Park Hotel, which I learned on recent enquiry to be still in business. I was then approaching the age of six and my brother the age of nine.

We spent happy, sunny days at a nearby swimming pool and loved to watch the monkeys cavorting freely everywhere. As children, we were quite unaware of the terrible events farther north. We were only interested in immediate concerns, like having after our children's early supper at the hotel a delicious dessert called *gula malacca* made, I believe, of freshly grated coconut and sweet molasses.

We then went to live in a rented house with Mother's twin sister and our grandmother. The house had two bathrooms, both on the ground floor—one best bathroom with white tiles and modern fittings and one second-best, rather grubby-looking, bathroom with uneven, lurid yellow tiling. Children were allotted use of the latter.

Happily, the arrangement did not last long. First, a tarantula was found one morning sitting on our toilet seat and had to be disposed of; then a few days later, a baby cobra was found on the floor of the bathroom and met a similar fate, this time involving golf clubs and much commotion. I was intrigued by the disappearance overnight of the body of the snake from where it had been thrown into the courtyard outside and was told that the ants had devoured it. After those two scares, we were allowed to use the adults' bathroom, a great improvement. For as long as we remained at that house, we were forbidden to go near some long grass at the end of the garden where it was feared that other similar creatures might be living, harmlessly so long as they were undisturbed.

In early 1938, when the situation in Shanghai was considered to be safer, we rejoined our father there in the house in Sinza Road.

Back in Shanghai

Life for the expatriate community in Shanghai during the early years of the European war, as it was experienced by a young boy of about the same age as my brother, has been well depicted by the author

J. G. Ballard in the opening pages of his autobiographical novel, *Empire of the Sun*[2]. Already in 1938, the adults were in a state of anxiety and uncertainty because of the imminent prospect of war in Europe; yet those still there in 1941 continued the same round of dinners and social gatherings at the Country Club, with the same succession of children's parties. Any who had remained when Japan attacked Pearl Harbor and fully entered World War II would be interned for its duration, as the young J. G. Ballard was—and as was Miss Phillips. The latter told me much later, without going into detail, that the experience had not been pleasant; however, in due course, she returned to England and pursued her career as a librarian in the city of Bath, living well into her eighties.

To England, 1939

In January 1939, when my brother was ten and I just seven, it was decided that Leslie should go to England to attend a junior boarding school. Mother and I would accompany him to England and stay there for a few months while our father stayed in Shanghai.

We left Shanghai on sixth March that year, and I clearly remember the parting with Father as our ship pulled away from the dock. As was customary, those on the quay who were seeing people off held one end of a colored-paper streamer while those on board held the other end. It was a colorful and touching scene for there were hundreds of these streamers, which broke, one by one, as everyone gazed intently at their loved ones on the dockside becoming more and more distant until they were lost to sight.

It took us exactly a month to reach the port of Liverpool in northwest England. First, we sailed slowly from Shanghai south

---

2. Ballard, J.G., *Empire of the Sun*, first published by Gollancz, 1984. Various editions available.

along the coast of China to Hong Kong. The ship stopped at several ports, and at each one the local authorities came on board and insisted on revaccinating everyone against smallpox. The captain of that coaster had two cocker spaniels, which he loudly and unabashedly called Wallah and Wallah Wallah. Every time he called for one of them both sat up expectantly; then one or the other would subside, much to our childish delight.

After a short stay in Hong Kong we embarked again on another ship for Kobe, Japan. There we stayed in a large hotel, and were shown around town by a kind Japanese lady who was the wife of a business friend of our Shanghai grandfather. I can remember being taken to a beautiful park, with gravel paths leading to elegant pavilions, which were, I think, made of wood; and to a large store, which specialized in exquisite silks of every conceivable color. Wherever we went we were fascinated by the grace and beauty of the Japanese women in their kimonos.

On one of our few days in Kobe we could not go out of the hotel at all. The town was struck by a full-scale typhoon, which lasted for the best part of a day and a night. We were not in danger in our solid, stone-built, shuttered hotel but through the slits in the shutters we could see the havoc being wrought on less solid structures on the other side of the street, and the extraordinary spectacle of not just bicycles but whole motor vehicles tumbling headlong, blown by the gale. Everyone became very tense and it was a great relief when the storm died down and calm was restored.

At Kobe, we embarked on a large oceangoing liner (the *Empress of Russia)* on which we crossed the Pacific Ocean to Vancouver. There we were met by a gentle, elderly woman—again, a friend of our China grandparents. She took us to her home on Vancouver Island where we spent pleasant days being delightfully spoiled. Since we were still in the month of March, everything was blanketed in snow and the air was crisp and dry. No doubt as a result, our hostess gave a little jump every time I had occasion to kiss her and complained that I had given her an electric shock. No one else in the party had this effect on her and I was not sure whether to be proud or rather embarrassed.

Soon—too soon—we left for the mainland and boarded a train on the Canadian Pacific Railway to cross the North American continent to Montreal. I think the journey took about four days. As we were passing through the Rocky Mountains, all were expecting to see a spectacular waterfall at a famous Kicking Horse Canyon. Many passengers, including the three of us, walked cheerfully to the rear of the long train where there was an open observation car. We waited in eager anticipation for the great moment and—nothing! There was no waterfall that day; everything was dried up and everyone just tramped back along the train to their rooms.

My brother must have been reading something about prairie fires. In the way of brothers, he loved to tease his gullible young sister so one night as the train was crossing the wide, flat expanse of the prairies, he pointed to a small glow of fire some way away in the darkness, probably somebody's brazier. "Look!" he said, "A fire! Do you know how quickly a prairie fire can spread? This train had better hurry!" I lay in my bunk looking through the window and keeping an eye on that small point of light, fearing the worst, until at last it disappeared from sight and I could fall asleep.

We enjoyed the new experience of our time on that train. Meals were lavish and varied and Leslie in particular rejoiced in the free availability in the dining car of fresh, creamy milk. This was something not obtainable in Shanghai, and he must have consumed gallons of it.

From Montreal, we took another train to St. John, New Brunswick, and from there, we took a slow, local train that chugged for an entire day along the north shore of the Bay of Fundy, stopping everywhere, to reach Halifax, Nova Scotia, where we embarked on another liner (this time, *The Duchess of York)* to cross the Atlantic to Liverpool.

Our mother managed all this traveling and changing between ships and trains, with baggage to look after and only the willing help and support of a ten-year-old boy and with me in tow. Even so, amid all the hustle and bustle of boarding a liner, she always remembered to put her hands over my ears whenever the deep roar of the ship's horn signaled departure, for otherwise I would be reduced to tears by the pain that sound caused to my young ears. Many people may not realize how painful such very loud, low sounds can be for an infant or young child.

Across the Atlantic to Liverpool

Mother and I were never good sailors, while the men of the family never experienced seasickness in any conditions. Soon after our ship left Halifax we hit very rough seas and, occupying myself alone in a playroom, I began to feel the effects. Motion sickness pills were not yet available; they came much later. Making my way back to our cabin, hanging onto anything available to stay upright, I met a kindly ship's officer who asked me if all was well. I told him I was feeling very funny! He was most understanding and helped me to reach our cabin before anything embarrassing happened. There I found Mother lying in her bunk, trying to weather the storm without throwing up, and we two stayed prone, unable even to think of food for a couple of days, while Leslie went on enjoying himself and making full use of the half-depopulated dining rooms.

The only other memory I have of that crossing is of the ship slowly making its way through ice and of seeing, not porpoises here as in the Pacific, but seals. Near them we spotted one cute, white baby seal sitting by itself on the ice. Leslie excitedly aimed his Baby Brownie camera and took a photograph of it but when the film was developed all we could see was the baby seal's nose, a black dot in a sea of whiteness. Before long our liner docked in the northwest English port of Liverpool.

CHAPTER TWO

England, 1939–'49

Having reached Liverpool on April 6, 1939, we went south to stay with Mother's twin sister, her husband and their young son in the county of Surrey. This was our first stop in what was to be for us a very unsettled existence for years. Mother and I were meant to return to China before the end of the year but the outbreak of war intervened and our plans were changed.

Our uncle had just returned to England from West Africa where he had been employed as an engineer. Very soon the house in Surrey was sold and a small cider factory near Wellington, in the southwestern county of Somerset, was bought instead; this had all the necessary machinery, its own apple orchards and a dwelling house on the premises as well. The product was a delicious, sweet, very alcoholic cider with the brand name Lorna Doone. Eventually that factory lost its independence to one of the two big Somerset cider-producing companies and Lorna Doone cider disappeared forever.

By early summer we had all moved to Somerset so that Uncle could start work in the factory. The house was not yet available so we took up residence for the time being in tents in a nearby field. For children like us from a big city, for whom even a dandelion or stinging nettle was a novelty, this was really fun. The summer weather was perfect and we reveled in the scent of the lush, grassy field and the feeling of freedom in the sun and open air. There was one very large tent that Uncle had brought with him from Africa; this became the center of activities and included sleeping accommodation for the adults. There were four smaller tents, one for the two boys, one for me, a store tent and a tent for a camp toilet—a perfect little encampment.

Eventually the inevitable happened, the fine weather broke and one night there was a violent thunderstorm. Everything was soaked and by next morning the grassy field was reduced to soggy mud. However two small tents that had collapsed were soon retrieved and put up again, things dried out and life continued as before. We bought fresh eggs and milk from the farmer who owned the field and the adults exercised all their ingenuity in devising methods of battling our then chief enemy—the wasps.

World War II Begins

This idyllic episode went on till, war being imminent, enthusiastic, newly appointed air-raid authorities stepped in to disrupt it. They came to our camp and said we must pack up and go, because our tents were not camouflaged and we would be a target for enemy bombers that would soon be passing overhead on their way to bomb Exeter and other west country cities. No argument was possible and the grown-ups had to scramble to find other accommodation in an already very crowded housing market.

What they found was an ancient two-up two-down cottage near a wood. The floors were as uneven as rough seas, the plumbing was beyond rudimentary, but it was a roof over our heads. This new temporary home was called Addlehole Cottage. As children we adjusted almost instantly and I remember no inclination on our part to complain. We went off cheerfully into the adjoining woods, armed with trowels, etc., to deal with routine calls of nature—there being no practical alternative—and I do not think we were aware of any particular hardship. For the adults, it may have been more trying.

My brother had soon to face a tougher prospect: he was equipped and name-taped and sent off to his school, where he had some unhappy times and, world traveler that he was, found most of the other boys of his age oddly childish. Our six-year-old cousin, Andrew, and I were sent temporarily to a small, local school where I learned to master joined-up writing, a skill perhaps less valued now than it was then. That was school number two. We only stayed for one term since the Addlehole Cottage arrangement was short-lived. School number three was to follow soon after, when there was yet another move and Mother and I were staying for a few months with Mother's parents in Sidmouth, a seaside town in Devonshire.

One clear memory I have from about this time is of the intensity of Mother's reaction when the Prime Minister, Neville Chamberlain, declared war on Germany following the invasion of Poland. That was the only occasion in my entire life when I saw my mother in tears. Her husband was on the other side of the world; we had no home of our own in England and only just enough money to get by. For her the prospect must have been particularly daunting.

Our family never did have a home of our own in England until Father, who had been in Chengdu, Western China, as the Royal Air Force's liaison officer with the Chinese Air Force there during World War II, and had afterwards returned to Shanghai to see if it was possible to pick up the threads of his career, accepted a small payoff from the Chinese government—just before the Communist Party took over—and on his return to England in 1948 bought a modest smallholding in Sussex.

Back to 1939

Soon we moved again to stay with yet more relations, this time on our father's side, in their home high on a hill above the picturesque Devonshire village of Lustleigh. Unfortunately for me, soon after we arrived there one of my cousins, Meg, came down with scarlet fever. This development inadvertently ushered in for me a year of confusion and darkly painful memories. At barely three days' notice, I was packed off aged eight to a nearby boarding school called Stover. For this sudden, new upheaval in my young life I was quite unprepared.

Here Be Dragons

Stover is a fine building in a beautiful location, which I was able for the first time to appreciate many years later when I was passing by and decided to stop and take a look at it. As a child there, I was lost. I could more or less understand what went on in the classroom but little else. On the day of my arrival, greatly daunted by the cold, stone stairs leading to my dormitory, I was overcome with homesickness and cried bitterly; whereupon a "matron" whose job it was to look after us scolded me furiously for upsetting another new girl who had arrived the day before and was a year younger than I was. The system of wartime rationing was not yet fully in operation and one result was that candies were almost unobtainable. As retribution for crying and thereby setting off renewed tears in the younger girl, the matron confiscated a can of peppermint chews someone had somehow found for me to take to school and said she was giving them to her. That low blow set the tone for much that would follow.

This matron seemed to me to have little warmth or loving kindness and since she was mostly in charge of us young ones when we were out of class, she contributed mightily to the dismal memories I have of my year at school number four. Comically, she may have had some conscience about her unfriendliness since she made much of being responsible for my being chosen as Chief Angel for a show the school put on at Christmas! The angels only had to stand still on tables at the back of a tableau, wearing white sheets and adorned with gold paper haloes and wings, so if I was in my usual state of bewilderment it hardly mattered.

Making a Run for It

During the following summer term there were one or two instances of girls running away from the school. My special friend at the time was a girl called Audrey who had the unusual distinction of possessing a glass eye, which, as a favor, she would take out and show to selected classmates. Audrey and I decided it would be a good idea to see if we too could escape.

We set off one sunny morning on the road towards Exeter, with the haziest of ideas about what we would do when we got there since we had hardly any money. Fortunately or unfortunately, our absence was soon detected and we were overtaken by an assistant teacher on her bicycle. We ran off into some woods by the side of the road to escape but it was no good. We had to go back to the school and were taken to see the head, a seemingly vague but kindly woman named Miss Dence. She rebuked us and dispatched us to separate rooms in the sanatorium to spend the day and a night contemplating our misdeed on a punitive diet of bread and water. Our luck was in, however.

It was the dreaded matron's day off and the kitchen staff, who clearly sympathized with us, brought us on trays the fanciest meals we ever had at Stover.

Mother took a quite indulgent view of this copycat escapade, thinking that at least it showed some spirit of enterprise. Father—who, being above the age to be enlisted, had come briefly to England to join the Royal Air Force Volunteer Reserve—took a sterner view. Sweet natured though he was, he believed in the stiff upper lip and in his view running away from anything was not to be encouraged.

Clearly Mother's view prevailed, for I was removed from Stover and placed in a smaller school for girls up to the age of thirteen. This school, called Rookesbury Park, had been moved from its usual premises in Hampshire to Haccombe House, a large, historic house in Devonshire, which was later converted into luxury apartments. All the private schools along the southeast and south coasts of England were evacuated at the outbreak of war to areas which were believed to be safer from the threat of the invasion everyone thought was coming. My brother's junior school was evacuated from Winchester to Blair Castle in Perthshire, Scotland. Meanwhile, trainloads of young children from the big cities were being wrenched from their families and sent to stay with willing strangers who lived outside the areas of immediate danger, and many others were sent to Canada or the United States. I was far from being the only child in England who was uprooted during that year.

Rookesbury Park School

I was at Rookesbury Park School as a boarder from the ages of nine to thirteen and, while the experience was sometimes turbulent owing to my own talkative nature—I used, for example, to read popular adventure stories by day and relay them to my dormitory at night, so

I was almost always the culprit caught talking after lights-out—it was a generally helpful and formative time.

The presiding genius was the owner and head of the school, a remarkable woman called Eileen Glenday who taught us Latin and Scripture. She was a large, no-nonsense person, who kept her straight hair in an unruly bun at the back of her head; her hobby was gardening, and we often saw her bent over, digging in her garden on the side of a hill near the house. I was in awe of her but loved her dearly, for I had complete confidence in her fundamental benevolence.

Miss Glenday made the young girls in the school experience the war and its austerities in a spirit of solidarity with the war effort; (an example of our imagined austerities: soggy Yorkshire pudding made with powdered eggs brought at great hazard across the Atlantic from the United States and leavened with great lumps of soda). She would call all the girls down in their nightclothes to her large study to sit on the carpet and listen to Winston Churchill's wartime speeches as they were made and broadcast on the radio, or "wireless". There were also several nights when we were roused from our beds and led down by candlelight to rest on straw-filled mattresses on the cobbled floors of the old cellars, which served as a makeshift air-raid shelter; this was not comfortable but we found it quite exciting. Though the sound of bombers overhead was familiar to all of us we were not the target and, so far as I know, no stray bombs fell near Haccombe House.

At Miss Glenday's school we were allowed to keep small pets in cages and were also given small patches of land on which we could grow whatever we liked. While not a keen or conscientious gardener I did have a large and handsome pet rabbit, whom I called Benjy. Hammering away with staples and nails, fixing chicken wire and workable doors to old, wooden boxes and crates, I made his living quarters and traveling box myself. Over the years, Benjy became a much traveled rabbit.

At Haccombe House, a common punishment for wrongdoing was to be told to walk up and down the length of a graveled courtyard in front of the house for half an hour. In my case they sometimes tried to mend my ways by also forbidding me to feed poor Benjy. Fortunately, since Benjy's cage was in a covered walkway at one end of the courtyard, stopping to slip him something to eat when no one was looking was entirely possible. When I moved on to the next or senior school, which did not allow pets, Mother took on the task of looking after Benjy. However, rabbit memories being short, after one school term he bit me when I came home and tried to pick him up. Luckily there was a rabbit farm near our home; Benjy was taken there and reportedly fathered astonishing numbers of offspring even by rabbit standards—possibly making up for lost time.

During our early years at boarding schools, my brother and I did not know until the last moment where we would be spending the holidays. Somehow our mother made some arrangement somewhere every time. Once we went to a hotel in Devonshire near the beautiful river Dart, where she had taken a job, but her health was undermined by the extended hours of work and she had to give that up. Before we eventually settled for a while with Mother's youngest sister and her family in a rented house called Chipley Cottage, which was within cycling distance of the cider factory in Somerset, Mother usually again stayed during the school terms with our Aunt Iris in Lustleigh. We had two aunts with homes in Lustleigh, a village famous for its picturesque, old thatched cottages; both were our father's sisters.

Just near the house to which Miss Glenday's school was evacuated was a small, old family church, its interior full of memorials to members of the aristocratic Carew family, going back many centuries. During my last term at the school, my Confirmation according to the Church of England took place in that church. We had to wear white head veils, a custom now generally and sensibly abandoned since those veils had a tendency to slip off and were nothing but a distraction. When we all knelt before the altar and the presiding bishop went along the line as usual, placing his hand on each girl's head, he leaned on mine so heavily that any chance of a moment of epiphany was lost for it was all I could do to keep my head upright on my neck. I was very disappointed by that and also because my mother had not turned up for the ceremony as expected.

Mother eventually arrived, just after everybody had left the church. She came in a car driven by Aunt Iris, a much-loved and respected character who was, however, known to be almost always late for everything. On this occasion the lateness was easily explained. They had managed to save up enough precious, rationed petrol but just as they were setting off from home the front passenger's door of my aunt's ancient car had fallen off. They had done their best to fix it, without success, and at last they came chugging up to the school with no door on my mother's side. I do not know if it was lawful—I am sure it would not be so today—but it was a noble effort and I was overjoyed to see them.

Chipley Cottage, 1944–'45

The shared household at Chipley Cottage, briefly mentioned above as being for a while a more settled home for our school holidays, included a Chinese woman known as an *amah*. The equivalent word in India is *ayah*. Amah had accompanied our mother's youngest sister, who was then pregnant with her fourth child, and her three children on board the *Duchess of Bedford*, which was the last passenger ship to leave Singapore before it fell to the Japanese. The entire group had been allocated little more than the space of a blanket on the deck of the ship as their accommodation for the long journey to England. Amah, as may be imagined, made superb Chinese food for us, besides helping to look after the baby who was born soon after we moved into this new home. She stayed in England for the rest of the war and then decided to return to China. When he returned to Shanghai in 1946 Father sought out Amah to see if she needed help, but after he finally left China we never knew what became of her.

At Chipley Cottage we children found many ways of amusing ourselves. This new home was surrounded by green fields and countryside that gave us plenty of scope for adventure. One favorite occupation was to pick our way carefully along the top of a high, old brick wall belonging to a nearby farmer. This wall was heavily overgrown with very old ivy; on one side one looked down on heaps of manure—since the wall surrounded a large cattle enclosure—while on the other there were tall banks of stinging nettles. We found this an absorbing and pleasurable challenge and it kept us happily occupied for hours.

While at Chipley Cottage too, we often rode our bicycles to the cider factory to play or, in season, to pick blackberries. Probably our parents—apart from Uncle Bob who was far too busy with his work to worry about it—never knew how much Lorna Doone cider we consumed whenever we were thirsty. I think I had a harder head for alcohol at the ages of eleven and twelve than ever again later in life.

My best friend during our time at Chipley Cottage was Gwen, the daughter of the above-mentioned farmer. She and I used to play at smoking Gwen's father's cigarettes, while comfortably ensconced in the straw stored in his large, two-storied barn—until one day I singed my eyebrow lighting up and Mother spotted it and put an end to the fun. They were good cigarettes, not then easy to come by, but if Gwen's father noticed some were missing I never heard that he made an issue of it.

There was one scary moment while I was playing in the barn with Gwen, though I only knew it was scary after the event. That was when I fell through a straw-covered hole in the upstairs floor of the barn. I was hanging there on my arms and elbows, convulsed with laughter and thinking that when I was ready the best thing to do might be to drop down to what I imagined would be more straw on the floor below. Gwen, who was downstairs at the time, came rushing up the stairs and hauled me out of the hole with great urgency. She had seen my feet dangling inches above the back of her father's very large, very bored and irascible bull, kept penned just below where I had fallen.

One summer holidays when we were about twelve, Gwen and I decided to do some good. We thought we would organize a fete, or garden sale, in aid of Dr. Barnardo's Homes for Children. We planned and worked on the project for weeks, buying with our pocket money or scrounging anything we could for the various stalls, and preparing the usual games and competitions. Then we decided we must also put on an entertainment; Gwen, who attended ballet classes, danced, and I sang an interminable song, with numerous verses, entitled "The Derby Ram." Everyone, adults and children, put up with our efforts with great patience and indulgence, and hearty—no doubt relieved—applause at the end. The whole thing was enthusiastically described by my brother in a letter to our father in Chengdu, which letter I discovered in our mother's sewing box after her death. We made the sum of five pounds sterling on that day, which was duly sent to Dr. Barnardo's and gratefully acknowledged. Grandfather King, who was then living in a hotel nearby, attended the function and I remember being much gratified by his approval, which was not always easily earned. No doubt he had a hand in the fact that our proceeds reached the round figure of five pounds, which, needless to say, was worth much more then than now.

We Move On Yet Again

I left school number five after the summer term of 1945. By then we were living with my mother's twin, Aunt Lesley, and her new husband-to-be, Bill Hunt; both were in the throes of divorce. Home was a picturesque, old, Elizabethan mill house close by a lake in the depths of the Sussex countryside. We had no electricity and little real plumbing, but again made the best of it. There was a chemical toilet which was emptied regularly by Uncle Bill with tuneful hilarity and some ribaldry, and baths were a heroic achievement. Sheffield Mill Farm, as this home was called, was situated on the edge of the Ashdown Forest. The beauty of its setting, with a running stream in front of the house and another larger one, fed from the lake through a sluice gate, behind it—and with the trees of the forest reflected in the lake in all seasons—amply made up for any lack of amenities.

Our aunt was never well off financially but she had the luck or destiny to marry two very amusing men. Uncle Bob when he was not working could be very entertaining, especially with children. Bill Hunt, who came from a distinguished Irish background, was shell-shocked and invalided out of the army when our aunt first met him—but nothing could suppress his extraordinary gift for creating laughter. He would hold forth at the dinner table about, for instance, his wartime army experiences in the Orkney Islands off the northern coast of Scotland and have us all laughing so much that we would beg him to stop. He was also a remarkable naturalist, who could spot a hare two fields away before the rest of us noticed a nearby rabbit. Later in life his talent as a raconteur found an outlet on Devonshire Radio, which must have brought his inimitable sense of humor into many other homes.

More Education

My last summer term at junior school was memorable for the celebrations in May of the end of the war in Europe. It was also the time for entrance examinations for our next schools. Faced with a Biology paper when we had only ever had lessons called Nature Study,

I offered "A Day in the Life of my Pet Rabbit" and always believed that that was how I got into my senior school, called St. Felix. Summoned in due course for interview at the school's wartime premises in Somerset, I attended with my mother, was pronounced by the Head to be "a friendly child", given an exhibition (less than a scholarship but still financially helpful) and accepted as a boarder for the following September. By that time the school would be back in its normal premises near Southwold, a small town on the east coast of England.

My mother made careful enquiries before deciding which boarding house I should join and finally selected one called Somerville because of the good things she heard about its housemistress. It was a good choice. The housemistress in question was a Scot, Miss E. K. McFarlane, who for some perverse reason was quite affectionately known by all the girls at the school as 'The Haybag'. No less apt name could have been chosen, for Miss McFarlane was always impeccably tidy with not a hair out of place. She was a tall, reserved, even shy woman, probably in her fifties, who had absolute integrity and a controlled streak of well-informed early feminism. I really liked and respected her.

I was at that school for the next four years. However schooldays are schooldays and mostly, despite all dramas theatrical and other, my time there was not particularly memorable. Being taken as a member of the school choir to the Royal Albert Hall in London to take part in a performance of the *St. Matthew Passion* by the nationally famous Bach Choir was one clear exception. The standard of music teaching at the school was very high.

One example if a non-theatrical drama while I was at the school was the following. After the public examinations were over towards the end of a Summer Term, three girls from another House called Gardiner slipped out one night and walked to the nearby seaside town of Southwold. They wore headscarves and pretended to be local young women intent on buying fish and chips. They got their fish and chips and seemed to have got away with their bold and irregular excursion too. One of my cousins who was also in Gardiner House and had left the school at the end of that term told me about this exploit when we met during the school holidays. She swore me to secrecy, of course, for the sake of her friends.

Soon after those of us who were staying on into the Sixth Form, a senior class, returned to school in the following September we were all summoned to the Head's study to hear, in the presence of all the housemistresses, about this brazen infringement of school rules. It had indeed reached the ears of the school authorities and the three girls concerned had been expelled.

"Now," said the Head, "I'd like to know how many of you knew this had happened."

All the Gardiner House hands went up and assuming I would be in good company I put my hand up too. Big mistake! All the others who had put up their hands were already known to have known, only my hand going up was a surprise. So much for following the pack and, no doubt, wanting to show one is in the know. There was a shocked silence; my dear Housemistress looked very upset and went dramatically red in the face and I was sternly asked by the Head why I had not brought this information to her. Of course, it had never occurred to me to do any such thing! I said I had been told about it in confidence during the holidays and anyway thought it was none of my business. Now I really was in trouble: my loyalty to the school was questionable and my judgment deplorably unsound. After that I might as well forget about aspiring to any leadership positions at the school, though eventually they did make me a school prefect since I stayed there for so long.

An odd incident which also occurred while I was in the Sixth Form at St. Felix School did nothing to help. There was in England at that time a well-known humorous writer and artist called Ronald Searle, whose specialty was illustrated stories about hockey-stick-wielding schoolgirls in gym slips, the dark-colored pleated tunics that were worn over a shirt, usually with a school tie. These schoolgirls were always completely anarchic and getting into chaotic scrapes which their distracted and bosomy teachers could never control.

One day a characteristic article by Ronald Searle appeared in a magazine called *Men Only* describing how a "smashing senior, Brenda Hancock" fainted during prayers at school because she had received a letter from her boyfriend, Humphrey. It was my misfortune that in the article every detail of Mr. Searle's imaginary girls' daily lives and terminology matched ours. The school authorities, who at that time were all women and not likely to be regular subscribers to *Men Only*, nevertheless came to know about this article and were deeply suspicious, thinking I must have put the author up to it. In fact I had never even met Mr. Searle—nor did I know who the real culprit was. Copies of that article were sent to me by several people; one even came from my cousin Andrew, who by then was in the British Merchant Navy in East Asia.

My time at St. Felix came to an end in December 1949. There is a twist in the story which came about much later. St. Felix was and is a good school but some of the rules and regulations while I was there seemed to me unnecessary and even irksome, though they were generally accepted at the time as being the way things were. When I was later involved in the founding of a girls' school, naturally I set out to avoid any such customary practices and to build instead as free a spirit as was compatible with the safe and efficient running of the school. It was, therefore, a source of quiet satisfaction to me when Anne Mustoe, a teacher and, later, author, whom I had originally appointed and who after I left became for a while our deputy head, went on to be the head of St. Felix.

CHAPTER THREE

Into the Wider World,
1950–'56

There was a general assumption that I would go on to university. I had set my sights on Newnham College, Cambridge, then a women's college, and stayed at school an extra term to prepare for the entrance examinations. My brother was still at Trinity Hall, having been delayed for two years by national service in the armed forces, then still compulsory for young men.

At Newnham, I was called for interview but then my luck ran out. The interviews were held in December after the end of the college term and the heating had been turned off. They were running very late, and I waited for an hour and a half, alone in a freezing room which became steadily darker. By the time I was called for the interview I was so benumbed and unresponsive that the interviewers must have wondered why they had ever considered me; and I was too overawed, and much too cold, to explain. So whatever might or might not otherwise have happened, Newnham College Cambridge was not for me.

As previously mentioned, our first real home in England was bought in 1948. While abroad during the war Father had dreamed of a quiet, rural life in England growing vegetables and flowers as a market gardener. He worked extremely hard and grew beautiful produce but could not market it to his advantage. We also had orchards, some chickens, pigs, and my mother had a Jersey cow so that we always had abundant milk and cream. In the end, however, they had to give it up; the property was sold and father obtained a temporary appointment in Nigeria. The British government was hiring older men as 'Administrative Assistants' in the run-up to Nigerian Independence and Father, as one of them, was posted to Ilorin, in the north.

Having missed my chance of a place at Newnham College I had to do something to retrieve the situation. From that first home in Sussex I therefore made a late application to enter for some scholarship examinations to colleges in London, since the ordinary admissions procedure for the following year had already been completed. The application was accepted and this time my luck held and I was given a scholarship. To the amusement of my delighted father it was called a '"Gamble" scholarship, after the name of the person who had endowed it. I spent an enjoyable term as an assistant teacher at Miss Glenday's school, now back in its home premises in Hampshire, and in October that year started a three-year degree course in Modern Languages at Bedford College, then still a women's college on a beautiful site in London's Regents Park.

Because of my father's difficult financial situation, the scholarship entitled me to receive a full state grant which took me through the degree course without burdening him at all. I was thus a—very grateful—beneficiary of the postwar welfare state in Britain, which in England at least is now much less generous to university students.

My maintenance grant while I was at college in 1950–1953 was £241 a year and with that one could manage quite adequately, even in London.

An advantage of being a student in London was the wealth of the city's cultural life. We made full use of the concert halls, theatres and opera. As students we always bought the cheapest seats; we had to climb innumerable stairs to reach the gods as those seats are popularly called, and though the angle of vision was odd one could see and hear everything.

One of my best friendships while at college came about through being elected as a member of the students' Union Committee. There were various roles committee members could choose and my choice was to be our liaison officer with an organization called the World University Service. The head at that time of this organization in London was Malcolm Joseph-Mitchell, a black man from Trinidad. Malcolm had earlier worked for the United Nations, investigating and reporting on the conditions of the aboriginal people in Australia. Now he worked for the WUS, distributing literature, running conferences, giving talks and organizing collection days. Malcolm was a tall man, a good deal older than me, with a very reassuring presence as he puffed away at a pipe filled with aromatic tobacco. We remained friends on and off for many years, and indirectly, our friendship helped to precipitate me into teaching, a career which I long resisted entering.

Abroad Again

My first solo trip abroad from England had started on April 6, 1939, ten years to the day after our arrival in Liverpool from China. I had been sent to Paris to stay for three weeks with a family who, while they knew English very well, obligingly spoke nothing but French whenever I was present. This first springtime visit to Paris was a delight which broke the barrier for me between stumbling schoolgirl French and reasonable fluency.

Later, as a student of languages, there were more opportunities to cross the Channel. Once, I spent a month with a family who lived in Amiens, supposedly earning my keep with some light work. My task was to help their nine-year-old son with his English, but my efforts were seriously obstructed by his feigned or real faith in his teacher at school. If we came across a word which in English was pronounced differently from the way he said his teacher had pronounced it, he maintained that I had no idea what I was talking about. After a couple of weeks, the family took me with them on holiday to the coast and the fruitless attempts at teaching English were abandoned.

At the end of the month I left by train for Bonn to attend a vacation course in German. The journey via Paris involved a further change of trains in Mainz and, this being 1951 and well before the days of the French fast-rail system, the train from Paris was many hours late. I missed my connection and found myself in the railway station at Mainz as night was falling. There were no more trains to Bonn that day, and I was exhausted, having been on the move since early morning.

I could not see a telephone so asked a magazine vendor where one might be. Having just spent a month talking French, I was finding it difficult to switch to German and my sentences tended to come out as a mixture of both languages. I could not make my request understood and eventually gave up on the magazine vendor and went into a busy restaurant where I asked a waiter. He caught the gist and directed me to a building round the corner outside the station. Past caring about it, I left my suitcase in the restaurant and went to look for the promised telephone.

Entering what I thought must be the building in question, I started to walk up some wide, marble stairs. There I was met by a distinguished-looking gray-haired man coming down. He asked me where I thought I was going! With difficulty I explained that I had missed my connection to Bonn and needed a telephone to find a hotel room for the night. He looked at me quite hard and said that no hotel rooms would be available in Mainz that night, since all of them had been taken by people attending a conference in the town. My heart plummeted, but mercifully he decided to help me. He accompanied me to the station where I retrieved my suitcase from the restaurant and together we walked the distance of about a block and a half to a small hotel.

I must have had the luck to run into someone of importance in the town, for this man spoke with great authority to the hotel management, saying that I was to have a certain room that was compulsorily kept for emergency use by officials, and specifying exactly what they might charge me. He shook my hand warmly and laughed aloud as I thanked him profusely in my mixture of German and French—and he was gone. Very soon I found myself in a clean, small room with a wash-hand basin and a comfortable bed and, thankfully, a very large key.

Next morning the sun was shining and the terrors of the previous evening were instantly dispelled. After checking out of the hotel, I made my way back to the station and onto a train to Bonn. It was a beautiful journey along the side of the river Rhine and past the famous Lorelei rocks. I knew I had had a narrow escape from a potentially ugly situation and felt that some higher power must surely have looked after me.

Touraine

The following year there was another language course, this time in the beautiful French region of Touraine. We were housed in a hostel in the city of Tours and the program of lectures was seasoned with day trips by coach to many of the famous *chateaux*. The group I was with was always accompanied by an enthusiastic and voluble guide whom everyone loved. He was a mine of historical information about all the places we visited.

This guide had a way of describing any unusual object or architectural gem as being *d'une valeur incontestable* so that before long we were all programmed to wait for that phrase to recur. He would cheerfully recount for us grizzly details from the past, pointing out, for example, where at the castle of Amboise (I think it was Amboise) unfortunate miscreants would be hanged from the castle wall overlooking the river Loire. On another occasion he showed us, with evident relish, a dark patch on the floor in the castle at Blois, saying that that was where the famous Duc de Guise had been murdered in 1588. We visited the castle of Chenonceaux, built across the river, which had served as a hospital during the 1914–'18 war. My favorite of all the *chateaux* we saw was the elegant moated Azay-le-Rideau, where we were taken for an evening performance of *son et lumière*.

One more trip to Europe later that year was to attend a United Nations-sponsored youth conference in Salzburg, Austria. It was just before Christmas; there was snow on the ground, the streets and shops were full of Christmas cheer and the beautiful, flood-lit castle seemed to float above the town at night. This was in 1952, however, and coming from England, it came as a shock to sense, more and more as one traveled east, the pervasive fear of a third world war. Indeed, the theme of the conference was the need for young people to work for a better, more peaceful future. We were also taken to visit the castle and Mozart's birthplace and childhood home, and one day went to see a small chapel and museum in the village of Oberndorf, a few miles outside the town. This was where, we were told, once during the previous century the church organ had failed just before Christmas and the priest and schoolmaster had composed at short notice the carol, "Stille Nacht" for the choirboys to sing accompanied only on the guitar.

Our final examinations at the university—since naturally college life consisted of more than concerts and theatres and vacation trips—coincided with the week of the coronation of Queen Elizabeth II in June 1953. Some of us went briefly to join the crowds in Oxford Street, but it was raining, and we could see very little, so we quickly withdrew. We had much else on our minds.

Attempts at Getting Started

Emerging from college with a bachelor's degree in Modern Languages, I found it qualified me for almost nothing. I was only sure that one of the most obvious choices for a female person at the time, teaching, was not for me. Various suggestions were made and investigated without positive result and eventually my mother gave me a hundred pounds with which to get myself trained as a shorthand typist, so that at least I could earn a living.

Sharing with a student friend a one-roomed apartment in a down-market part of south London I joined a course at a small secretarial college in Kensington and worked hard, knowing there could be no more money forthcoming. At the end of the three months, which were all I could afford, the college was kind enough to certify that I could manage speeds of a hundred words a minute in shorthand and forty-five a minute in typing. I had in fact worked at the course with something like desperation and was told that later groups of students were tired of hearing my name and being asked why, if I could do it in three months, they could not work faster—but probably they did not have the same incentive.

My first secretarial job was with an organization described as part of the Foreign Office, where everything was confidential and shorthand typists had to attend a quaintly named "Secs' course" so that we could learn how to be discreet. I think it was mainly designed to make us feel important and special. One day my World University Service friend from Trinidad rang the office and asked for me. A senior secretary happened to be in the room at the time, and something was said which indicated that my very good friend the caller was black. When shortly afterwards I had occasion to go to see the Chief Personnel Officer, and she left the room in response to some summons leaving her papers on her desk, naturally I took a look at what was on my card. There I saw, writ large by hand, the words "Coloured friends!". I knew at once that that meant I would not be given the non-European posting I was hoping for, and within two months I had left. That, of course, was in the early 1950s.

Questionable Business

Next, I found a job working for a woman who ran a small company in the West End of London near Regent Street, specializing in the wholesale purchase and sale at a discount of almost anything wanted by clients who were planning to go abroad. An eventual partnership was suggested as a possibility if all went well. An interesting aspect of this job was that it involved going to furniture factories and worksites in the East End and other parts of London that I had not previously had occasion to visit; I came to quite enjoy the cheerful wolf whistles coming my way! A big advantage of the job was that one met the clients, usually friendly and interesting people who were about to leave for various parts of the globe.

There was a snag, however. Many manufacturers then had a strict policy of retail price maintenance and they were very suspicious of my boss's activities—in truth, with ample justification. The business depended on carrying no stock and therefore being able to undercut the retailers. The crunch came when I was asked to write and sign a letter to a well-known company specializing in the manufacture of quality furnishing fabrics, declaring without a shred of truth that anything we bought from them would be sold to our clients at the normal retail price. I saw that this was not going to work and handed in my resignation—hours, I believe, before I would anyway have been fired for my reservations.

I took this turn of events philosophically, seeing it as just one of life's interesting experiences. Some years later, the practice in Britain of retail price maintenance became unlawful and manufacturers started to set recommended retail prices instead, which are binding on no one. If that had been the situation in 1954, my business career might have lasted a little longer.

It was while I was still engaged in this pleasant if slightly questionable business that I had one of those sudden moments of understanding that will stay with a person forever. This happened when I was sitting alone one sunny lunch hour in a London square not far from the office. Something so obvious dawned on me that I was surprised that it had not occurred to me before, namely, that we are immersed in our material world just as fish are in water, since the air we breathe has material substance and if it did not it would do our lungs no good to breathe it. For me at that moment this came as a seminal insight for it meant that, everything around us being perceived only through our bodily senses, things might not be in reality as they appeared to us to be. If at school I had not chosen languages over science, I might have come to that realization sooner.

My newly jobless situation was real enough, however, and out of a combination of necessity and indecision about what to do next, there followed a series of temporary secretarial posts.

Eureka!

To put it mildly, I was not much good at 'temping'. There were not yet even any word processors; multiple copies were made on type-writers with carbon paper and all mistakes, and I made many, had to be corrected manually on every copy. Before long I felt I could hardly bear to touch another piece of carbon paper. After a few months of this, I recalled one evening that I had been much more construc-tively engaged and much happier during my one term as an assistant teacher at my old junior school than in any job I had done since leaving college. At last resistance crumbled. I was suddenly fired up and pacing the floor of the small apartment I was sharing, firmly resolved on becoming a teacher.

I was working just then in the office of the Principal of London University. This was in one half of the Senate House which houses the administrative offices of the university; the other half housed the Institute of Education. Next day, I walked across to the Institute to try to enroll for the following academic year.

Teacher Training

Once again I was applying for something well past the closing date for applications, and once again the application was accepted. Summoned in due course for interview, I was waiting to be called when another late candidate sitting beside me asked me if I was in favor of the "direct method" of language teaching. I knew noth-ing about it at all and asked her what it was, whereupon she kindly explained in a few words what the direct method was. Basically, one demonstrates with actions the meaning of the words.

At the interview I was asked after a few preliminaries to show how I would teach the relative pronoun in French. I took two books of different colors that were lying on the table in front of me and, putting one back on the table and one on a chair, proceeded to demonstrate by means of the direct method how I would teach the relative pronoun! The interviewing panel beamed; the senior interviewer thumped the table and declared me a *born* teacher—and I was in. With luck like that I felt that perhaps I was on the right track at last.

After having a happy time producing a play, playing tennis, swimming, and attempting to teach a little French for a term at a small private school in the west of England, I started on the one-year postgraduate teacher-training course at the Institute of Education in October 1955. For the teaching practice segment of the course, which teachers will know can be a seriously challenging experience, I was sent to a county high school in Essex, rather a lucky choice. For the rest, while like many new graduates I had been quite ready to leave the academic world at the end of the first degree course, now I delighted in the return to life as a student and found myself reveling in the freedom to read voraciously, roaming well beyond the requirements of the course.

As a so-called mature student at age twenty-three, my year at the Institute was again financed by the State. The grant was conditional on one's teaching subsequently for at least two years at a school in England but during the course of that year the condition was for some reason revoked, though we were still expected to honor the intention of it. Accordingly, towards the end of the year I applied for several posts in and around London, without success. Feeling that I had done my best, I applied to the now-extinct Colonial Office in London in response to an advertisement for a teaching post at a school in Nairobi and was appointed for a four-year tour of duty there. In August 1956, in company with two other women newly appointed to government posts in East Africa, I set sail for Kenya.

CHAPTER FOUR

East Africa, 1956–'60

We were given the choice of traveling to Kenya by air or by sea. I had chosen to go by sea because I thought it would be more interesting, and so it turned out to be. Our Union Castle ship was one of the last to pass through the Suez Canal before the canal was rendered unnavigable by President Nasser of Egypt's decision to block it with scuttled vessels. Thereafter, for several years the sea route to Kenya would be via the southern tip of Africa.

The political situation was very tense as we entered the canal. Soon our ship and many others of all sorts and sizes were held up for a day and a night in the Great Bitter Lake. Nobody could be sure what was going to happen. However the scene was exceedingly beautiful as the sun went down that evening. Against the background of pink, blue and purple hills of sand, one by one all the ships began to light up and then, as night fell, the glittering lights of all those ships and their silhouettes presented an unforgettable sight. To general relief, next day we received the signal to move on and continued our journey through the Red Sea, past Aden and the Horn of Africa, and in due course arrived safely in the Kenyan port of Mombasa.

Arrival in Kenya

On disembarking, we three new government appointees took the train up-country to Nairobi. Fascinated by the unfamiliar scenes of the African bush through which we were passing, we all looked out of the window constantly until the light failed. I do not know what we expected but we were quite surprised when we went to the dining car and were offered a very English dinner of roast pork and applesauce. The colonial days were nearly over, but not quite yet in 1956.

In Nairobi my brother, who was by then nearing the end of a tour of duty in Kenya as a District Officer, was there at the station to welcome me. My traveling companions went their separate ways, and Leslie drove me to the school where we met the Head and were directed to my temporary living quarters. My four-year stint as a teacher in Nairobi had begun.

Education in Kenya

In 1956, the Kenya High School, which served some six hundred girls, all boarders and all of European descent, had I was told been listed in the previous year as eighth in the British Commonwealth for its standard of academic success. Reflecting no doubt some characteristic male disrespect for all things female, the school was known locally in the white community as the 'Heifer Boma' (a *boma* being a compound or enclosure). It was extremely well equipped, with all-brick buildings for both tuition and residential accommodation. There were laboratories, tennis courts, a large swimming pool, a dining-hall with a stage, big enough to cater for the whole school at one sitting—in fact, it was a fine institution. The Head, Miss Stott, had presided over the entire process of planning and building the school up. It was a Government of Kenya school, but the running of it was modeled largely on Westonbirt, a well-known private school for girls in the west of England.

My one regret was the segregated educational system in Kenya at the time. Girls of Asian descent could attend a school specially provided for them called the Duchess of Gloucester School, and outside Nairobi there was for Africans the Limuru School for Girls. There was a stark difference between the standard of facilities available for Africans and those provided for the Europeans. The same pattern was followed for the boys' schools.

In 1956, Kenya had just emerged from the Mau Mau uprising. There had been many ugly incidents, mainly in the remote areas of the so-called White Highlands, where settlers had made their farms. Africans as well as whites had been slaughtered. Jomo Kenyatta, the great Kenyan pre- and post-Independence leader, was still in detention far from Nairobi. The slow progress towards independence had no doubt begun, though it did not show on the surface. Apart from all other considerations, it was obvious that for the long term good of the best-equipped schools, if not for the country, it was necessary to open them to African and Asian pupils.

Miss Stott had great prestige with the government and among whites all over Kenya as an outstandingly successful school head. Once I was settled in the school and had responsibility for a House of fifty girls, I begged her to start the process of making the school multi-racial. I knew she was keen to do it but while I was at the school she never did. However in a letter she sent me in June 1961, after I had returned to England, Miss Stott recalled our conversations: "I wish your plans might direct you back to us now that we are becoming fully and successfully integrated with African and Asian girls." So it had started, and it had started in her time, which I found pleasing even if much overdue.

The Capricorn Africa Society

Colonel David Stirling, famous for his leadership of the British SAS, the Special Air Services, in North Africa during World War II, had founded an organization known as the Capricorn Africa Society. His main base was in Salisbury, now Harare, in Southern Rhodesia, now Zimbabwe. The Capricorn Africa Society had a branch in Nairobi, with which I quickly became associated. This branch was led by an eminent plastic surgeon, Michael Wood and his wife, Susan, whom I came to know quite well. The society helped to start a very good, small multi-racial primary school in Nairobi; its main object, however, was to advocate adoption of a system whereby every adult would be entitled to vote in political elections, but with more than one vote according to a set of agreed qualifications from which racial origin would be excluded.

The idea was a non-starter politically but these very good people were, so far as I knew, the only whites on the spot and familiar with local conditions who were publicly advocating any kind of political liberalization in East Africa at the time. Later in life, when my work involved the legal concept of indirect discrimination as it is understood in European Community law and in the British Sex Discrimination Act of 1975, I could see that the idea of such a system of multiple voting was a textbook example of that concept. Indirect discrimination consists of a policy or rule which on the surface appears to be evenhanded but which in practice works out disproportionately to the disadvantage of one affected group. Most white settlers in Kenya as in Rhodesia were anyway still in no mood to listen; in fact, it seemed to me that many had little time for what some liked to call 'people of your ilk', i.e., whites with liberal leanings.

At Work in the KHS

At the Kenya High School, besides teaching French and some German, I was co-opted to give two-weekly talks on current affairs to the assembled senior classes. There was no competition for this latter task, which I quite enjoyed. Regular classroom teaching was absorbing and could be fun but I welcomed the chance to awaken in that large group a broader interest in world and regional events than their usual daily preoccupations might allow. I was not content with classroom teaching alone, however, and before long, as already mentioned, was given responsibility also for a residential House.

This House was called Kerby. It had a very bad reputation when I took it over and I was told that during the previous school year there had been fighting there in the dormitories. If that was true, the troublemakers must have departed, for I liked the girls in the House—though they were short on leadership and seemed, if anything, a little depressed.

That was easily understood, since Kerby House so regularly came last in all competitions that the girls in all the other houses could feel sure that, whatever happened and however badly they did, Kerby would always be there as a face-saving cushion beneath them. At the school there was a system whereby, according to some elaborate method of earning points in schoolwork, sports and other inter-House activities, all the houses were listed according to merit at the end of each term and the one that came out on top was designated Cock House. This was always the last announcement, and caused great cheering and excitement—but hardly for poor Kerby. Over the months and years however Kerby House slowly picked up momentum, and it was pleasing to hear that the next term after I left Kenya and returned to England Kerby, to stunned silence followed by great applause and cheering, was named Cock House. The Head of House wrote and told me all about it!

My years with responsibility for a House at the Kenya High School gave me at an unusually young age invaluable experience and insight into the running of a large, secondary boarding school, not least through attendance at the head's weekly meetings with all the other house heads. This prepared me inwardly—gave me the confidence—to take on not long afterwards a headship of my own.

Using the Holidays

Teachers tend to claim that they need the school holidays in order to preserve their sanity. For many there is much preparatory work to be done during the holidays, but usually it leaves time for other activities as well, or none. I was able to make full use of the school holidays while based in Nairobi and could make some memorable journeys by car, ranging on different occasions from the north of Uganda to the southernmost part of what was then Tanganyika. Within months of my arrival, my brother observed that I had seen more of Africa than he had in years—though he made up for this when, on leaving Kenya at the end of his tour of duty, he drove west through central Africa to Nigeria to visit our parents in Ilorin.

It was still clear that something else was needed to make use of whatever free time I had beyond occasional touring around East Africa and socializing with friends and acquaintances. I therefore decided to study for the next qualification in Education offered by London University. After enrolling with a correspondence college in Oxford and opting for Educational Psychology as one of my special subjects, I found on investigating the public library in Nairobi not one book on any branch of psychology. Everything I needed had to be ordered from England and sent by mail via the Cape.

One day not long before the final examinations, I found on returning from some outing that my little dachshund, Tina, had pulled out of a bookcase and torn to shreds, page by page, almost the whole of the UK's Education Act 1944, at the time the most important piece of educational legislation in recent years. It would take months to replace it. I had finished my work with the Act, however, so could enjoy the joke of my dog unilaterally tearing up an Act of Parliament to register a protest. From then on I took her with me wherever I went and left her, if necessary, in the back of the car. With that arrangement she was content since in her view she had not been left behind.

In addition to the diploma studies, I had been for several years and still was at the time enrolled with a group based in New York, called the School for Esoteric Studies. This involved studying and writing papers mainly based on the books by Alice A. Bailey, who for her most substantial work took dictation from a Tibetan spiritual teacher by means of her rare gift of mental clairaudience. One was free to set one's own pace with the assignments, which would then be sent to more experienced people who might be anywhere in the world; I was in communication with a woman living in Northern Ireland. In Nairobi I also met some people of Indian origin who were enthusiastic devotees of Sri Aurobindo whose ashram was, and is, in Pondicherry (Puducherry). Seeing I was interested in what they were telling me, they showed me albums of photographs of Sri Aurobindo and his companion, known as The Mother. They also gave me a book, *Prayers and Meditations of the Mother,* a beautiful read, which I have with me still.

The elderly Church of England parson, whose classes of preparation for Confirmation I attended during my last term at junior school, gave a dry-as-dust introduction to church doctrine and practice but I did my best to accept it; I was young and wanted to be confirmed. As an adult I would still cheerfully enter "C. of E." on official forms as necessary but was not attached to any exclusive approach to truth and saw a clear distinction between Christ and the various forms of Christianity. In fact, from the day that my regular churchgoing father set me thinking as a teenager by confiding that he personally believed in reincarnation, the notion that "we only live once" has made no sense to me. I dropped the subject for a while after a particularly scathing putdown for mentioning it in a religious instruction class at school but it soon came back. Now these various studies and contacts while I was living and teaching in Nairobi meant that when, years later, I went to India I already had some basic familiarity with aspects of Indian and Tibetan thought and philosophy.

Flight to Embu

Apart from school work and these various other preoccupations, as already stated there was plenty of opportunity to explore and get out and about. My first trip from Nairobi had taken place within a few weeks of arriving there. My brother Leslie was a member of the Nairobi Aero Club and had decided to fly with me and a colleague, Rachel, whose cottage at the school I was temporarily sharing, to a place called Embu where we could all spend the day with friends. Now, my brother was six feet five inches tall, Rachel was just over six feet and I only a couple of inches shorter. This was a significant load for a small aero-club plane, probably a Tiger Moth, which appeared to be held together with canvas and glue.

All went well until Leslie tried to induce the plane to stop before the end of the bumpy Embu airstrip. It was not to be done. We came to a juddering halt nose first in a ditch with a bank behind it, which made it impossible for the plane to run on any further. Somewhat shaken, we all climbed out and went to inspect the propellers. They looked all right. The plane was very light and, my brother's friends having arrived on the scene to welcome us, with all hands helping it was soon out of the ditch. Leslie then decided to take the plane up for a trial flight to see if, later, we could return in it to Nairobi. There had been no obvious damage, and in the event the plane seemed to behave entirely as it should, so our intrepid pilot was satisfied and this time brought the plane to a halt without mishap.

Nevertheless, while nobody said anything, we were all looking down at the land beneath us, much of it dense forest, throughout the return journey. Those little planes might just fall out of the sky with all on board if anything went wrong, and we knew it. There was no question of parachutes. Until we were safely on the ground in Nairobi we could not be sure that there really was no structural damage or strain. Indeed, when they heard what had happened, the club authorities took the plane out of service for a thorough checkup before they would allow it to be flown again.

That was my first experience of flying, all my earlier travel having been by sea or land.

Further Roaming

Teachers at the school were eligible for a government loan at a low rate of interest for the purpose of buying a car; this was thought to be necessary because no public transport was available. I chose a Morris Minor 800 and in this small car made several long and eventful trips; it finally accompanied me to England, having been driven from Nairobi to Cape Town at the end of my four years in Kenya.

Soon after the end of my first term at the school I embarked with a new friend called Molly on my first exploratory tour of parts of East Africa. This was the trip that caused my brother to observe that in a short time I had seen more of the country than he had in years. Molly and I drove north through the Rift Valley and on past the Jinja dam and Kampala in Uganda towards Lake Albert, which borders the Congo. We went on as far as Gulu, the largest town in the Northern Province. On our way we frequently stopped to greet the local people and if they seemed happy about it took photographs of them and their homes. In Gulu we met some friendly Europeans who took us to see a tobacco factory and, just outside the town, a large Roman Catholic cathedral, very ornate and beautiful inside— surprising to see in such a remote part of the Northern Province of Uganda. On one of our days in Gulu, we all went to visit and climb a huge rock near the remains of Baker's Camp in a beautiful spot high on a hill; from there in the nineteenth century Sir Samuel Baker, who among many other attributes was an abolitionist, watched to intercept Arab slave traders.

On our way back south, we stopped at a township called Butiaba on the shore of Lake Albert and boarded a small steamer bound for the Murchison Falls on the Victoria Nile, which flows into the lake. We sailed in the evening; there were about five or six other passengers and as the sun was setting we were all served on deck an excellent fish dinner, prepared by hardworking people deep in the bowels of the ship. Afterwards, I went towards the bow and leaned on a railing to watch as night fell and the steamer chugged north towards the mouth of the river. Molly joined me for a few minutes but did not stay.

It is difficult to express the delight I felt that evening as I stood there alone. The cause was a magical display of light and darkness. As the last of the daylight faded the stars began to appear, looking huge above us. Far away to the east, an electric storm was silently lighting up the sky with great, pulsating flashes of sheet lightning. Meanwhile, the ship's pilot had a searchlight with which, every few moments, he scanned the blackness of the water ahead of us. I soon saw why: he was making sure we did not run into fishing nets, which could be spotted by the pieces of wood that kept their edges afloat. Once, the searchlight revealed a fisherman in his dugout canoe, out there alone in the darkness on the lake. Then, to complete the enchantment, as we approached the river the riverbanks were alight with millions of fireflies. At last I dragged myself away and went down to our tiny cabin where Molly had already settled in for the night, and fell asleep to the throb of the engines.

Next morning we rose early to watch for wild animals near the river bank as our steamer approached the falls. There were hippos, elephants, black-and-white monkeys and even a pair of rhinos, as well as many large, unfamiliar waterbirds. New to East Africa as we were all this was quite thrilling and fascinating to us. When it was time to disembark the whole party set off in single file, with armed *askaris* at the front and rear of the line; we were told this was a precaution against wild elephants. As we walked in the early morning sunshine on a narrow footpath towards the falls we could sometimes glimpse them ahead of us. Mostly we walked uphill but at one point the path descended again almost to river level, where we crossed a raised wooden walkway within two or three feet of many basking crocodiles. Then the path led steeply up again and we were at the top near the falls.

The gorge was quite narrow and the water must have fallen about 150 feet. The river was in spate when we were there; we were told that that was our good luck since at other times the falls, with surging waters now and rainbows produced by the sun shining on the spray above them, were less spectacular. After all had had a chance to absorb the scene and take photographs from various vantage points, we retraced our steps to the steamer, which took us back to Lake Albert to continue its journey northward.

This time we had a good view from the lake of the (then) Belgian Congo to the west as we headed towards the steamer's final port of call, a town called Packwach. Happily our stop there was short, since we found the town hot and uninspiring. Apparently we had just missed the most exciting event in Packwach in years, since an oil tanker and ferry had foundered there the day before and that was all anyone was talking about. We made our way back to our steamer as quickly as we could in the heat. By next day we were back in Butiaba, back in the car and driving south towards Fort Portal—through a veritable snowstorm of butterflies that continued for many miles.

At Fort Portal, we had the pleasure of staying for a night at the Mountains of the Moon Hotel, from which we could set out in the morning to explore the Queen Elizabeth National Park. At various points along our route signs had been put up announcing that "Elephants have Right of Way", while others told us when we crossed the equator. Of course, those signs were for the benefit of tourists like us, and of course, we reacted as expected with our cameras. We also saw and photographed many more wild animals, the most notable being a beautiful waterbuck standing alone and looking at us momentarily before it swiftly bounded away out of sight.

That trip included a spectacularly beautiful drive through the Rwenzori Mountains into the eastern limits of the Congo in an unsuccessful attempt to see gorillas, though we did catch a rare glimpse of a leopard as it crossed our path in broad daylight. Our furthest point on this trip was a small town called Bukoba, in Tanganyika on the western bank of Lake Victoria, where we had been invited to spend a few days relaxing with friends of friends. There the hippos wandered freely in the streets and gardens at night, snorting and grunting noisily and leaving deep footprints wherever they went.

There were other trips, to the coast, to different destinations up-country, and one long trip to Mbeya, in southern Tanganyika on the border of what is now Malawi to visit Zoë, a community relations officer with whom I had traveled on the ship to Mombasa. Once I spent two wonderful weeks with Susan and Michael Wood and their family at their farm on the northern slopes of Mount Kilimanjaro. There the night visitors to the garden were not hippos, but elephants. We traveled to the farm from Nairobi in Michael's plane, which he used for his personal no-charge "flying doctor" work among the

African population. It was fascinating to look down and watch the large herds of zebra, wildebeest, buck and other wild animals reacting below to the sound of the small plane's engine.

Last Days at the KHS

My four years at the Kenya High School were completed at the end of July 1960. I was to return to England by sea from Cape Town and for many weeks had been planning with yet another friend the long drive from Nairobi, making overnight bookings for the remote areas and arranging many meetings with friends or friends of friends along the way. We allowed ourselves two months for the journey.

In the event, my break with the school was abrupt and without ceremony, for that year the girls were suddenly sent home early to make room for hundreds of Belgian refugees from the Congo, where there had been a violent rebellion. The severely injured were sent to Brussels by air immediately but our school acted as a hostel and clearinghouse for many others. It was a large-scale rescue operation carried out by the Kenya government, with the help of numerous volunteers.

Busloads of refugees, men, women and children, drove up to the school. As a French speaker I was kept very busy, receiving and interpreting for these tired, uprooted people, who had lost everything and were mostly still in shock. Whatever the colonial history of the Congo, these people were in desperate need of help and we did our best to help them.

Some of the refugees with whom I spoke expressed as much astonishment as appreciation of the scale of the operation being carried out on their behalf; one even observed to me that if the roles had been reversed, he doubted if they would have done the same for us! When I was due to leave with Penny, a secretary at the school, on our long journey south, many refugees were still in residence; however helpers were numerous and my work on reception had ended, so we stuck to our schedule.

Believing that guns attract guns, and having anyway no experience with guns, I armed myself and Penny before we set out with a bottle of ammonia, which I had had carefully diluted by a pharmacist in Nairobi to surprise and embarrass without inflicting lasting damage to the eyes of animals or people. The idea was that, since it was colorless, the ammonia would look like water until it was tossed. I placed it on a shelf under the steering wheel, and two days out of Nairobi, we threw it out of the car because the lid was leaking and the ammonia was making our own eyes water. In any case, although we had to drive near the southern tip of the Congo, and although parts of Bulawayo, which was on our itinerary, were burned in an uprising just before we left, we never had need of a weapon.

The last evening before we left Nairobi, I met for the first time a man associated with the London office of the Capricorn Africa Society, of whom I had often heard during the preceding months and years. After his visit to the society in Nairobi, he was going on to Salisbury (now Harare) and we made a plan to meet again there.

Journey South

This journey, as we know, took place in 1960. Nowadays, most of the countries we passed through are known by names of their own choosing instead of those given to them by the British. It would be anachronistic to use the modern names in this account however, and tedious to continue giving both names. Therefore, after the first mention of a town or territory I have generally used the name by which it was known at the time.

Our first destination was Dar-es-Salaam, on the coast of Tanganyika. This was before Tanganyika and Zanzibar were united to become Tanzania. In Dar, we were made welcome by the parents of a girl in Kerby House, who put us up for the night and helped us to place the car in a reliable garage for servicing. We then took a short flight to Zanzibar to visit that extraordinarily beautiful island for a couple of days.

Zanzibar must be one of the most photogenic places anywhere and it was quite frustrating that I had left my camera in the car when we took it to be serviced. However we enjoyed exploring the town with its elaborately carved doorways, its vendors of aromatic spices and other signs of Arab influence. Zanzibar was also a free port, and there were in particular many jewelry shops, which offered very reasonable deals. We spent our one evening in Zanzibar walking along the sandy, palm-fringed beaches, enjoying the warm sea breeze and the play of the moonlight on the sea. On our return to Dar-es-Salaam, we found the camera safe in the car where I had left it.

Our route then took us due west into the center of Tanganyika, through beautiful, hilly country with a river running far below us. After we reached the inland town of Dodoma, which was not then but is now the country's official capital, we could swing round and follow the roads to the south. We briefly visited again my shipboard friend, Zoë, in southern Tanganyika and then drove on through many, many miles of bush country in Northern Rhodesia (Zambia), frequently for long stretches seeing no human habitation at all until we approached the capital, Lusaka.

Here we suddenly found ourselves driving on tarmac, first on strips and then on a fully tarred road. Soon we were in a busy town, with cars parked along the sides of the road, traffic and shops and people going about their business and shopping. It was almost a shock to reenter such a scene of bustle and activity. We stopped in Lusaka for a couple of days, relaxing and enjoying the contrast with the lonely trek through the African bush, then set off again towards

Livingstone and the Victoria Falls—in the local language "the Smoke that Thunders." The falls were, of course, fully as impressive as we had been led to expect. We stood for a long time, appreciating their sheer scale and power, again admiring the rainbows the sun made in the spray, and listening to the roar of the falling water. No ordinary camera could do the scene justice.

At Livingstone we once more took the opportunity to have the car serviced. And then, almost as soon as we left the township, we had our first breakdown. A man in a passing car going towards the falls offered to help and contacted the garage for us to ask someone to come out and see what was wrong. Luckily, we were only about a mile and a half out of town. The mechanic who arrived was quite flustered, since it was he who had done the work on the car; however, he probably could not have foreseen that the fuel pump was about to fail and as for us, we were only grateful for his help. Soon a new pump was fitted and we were on our way to the Southern Rhodesian (Zimbabwean) border.

Into Southern Rhodesia

Arriving in Bulawayo, we sought out Jack, a colleague's friend whom she had asked us to meet. We stayed in a hotel and spent a day or two with Jack, seeing around the locality including the recently damaged parts of the town. Jack then said he was anyway going to Salisbury/ Harare and would drive there in convoy with us in his own car. He was knowledgeable and cheerful and it was good to have his company.

As we approached Salisbury, we began to have more car trouble and, while the car was being fixed in the city, we all three took a day-trip north again by air to see the Kariba Dam, which had just been completed. This was a huge structure and we were given a very informative conducted tour of its technological marvels—absorbingly interesting at the time but their details by now long forgotten. Next, we were taken in a motorboat onto the lake, which was in the process of being filled. We took photographs of the tops of trees, which could be seen just above the level of the water; in one more day they would disappear forever. We were told that the wild animals had been rounded up and taken to safety before the land was flooded.

We were extraordinarily blessed with that small Morris car. We had spent many days driving through unpopulated bush country and the first breakdown happened close to a township, while the second started just before we reached Salisbury. When we took the car to a garage for repair, we were told that something called the big end had to be replaced. I had no idea what that meant and I do not think Penny knew any more than I did but if it was going to happen it could hardly have happened at a more opportune time.

We spent two more days in Salisbury; on one of them Jack took us to watch the tobacco auctions, which were conducted at tremendous speed in a sort of singsong vernacular incomprehensible to an outsider. Then with the car back in action, we said good-bye to Jack and were off again towards the Zimbabwe Ruins, not far from the border with South Africa. These ruins, believed to date from the eleventh century, are the remains of large, drystone structures indicative of a past civilization whose history is largely unrecorded. I remember in particular a tall conical tower which appeared to be almost intact; one was left wondering what its purpose might have been. No doubt it was from these ruins that the modern name of Zimbabwe was derived.

Into South Africa

As soon as we passed through customs and immigration at Beit Bridge into the Union of South Africa, we found the roads fully tarred and driving much easier. We had now left behind the dirt roads with their surface corrugations and trailing clouds of red dust. We were soon struck by the sheer beauty of the countryside and the vistas that stretched out before us. We were very aware that this was the land of *apartheid* but had not known quite how blessed it was with natural beauty.

In our planning, Penny and I had allowed one week each for Johannesburg, Durban and Cape Town. We had made and would make other stops but these three were the longest. We mostly stayed in hotels and in the big cities parked the car and went around by public transport or on foot.

In South Africa then, all doors opened for you if you were white. This happened so smoothly and seemingly naturally that even though we had heard and read about the prevailing political and social system, it could be all too easy to forget that for the majority of the population life was very, very different. So much was hidden from view.

For example, when we were in Johannesburg, we were taken on an organized visit to a gold mine. The visit was smoothly and efficiently conducted and everybody was very nice to us. We learned, however, that most of the miners we saw came from countries further north, without their families, to earn money to send home. They were provided with basic bachelor accommodation while they worked at the mine. Working in a mine is tough anywhere; however one sensed an atmosphere of controlled unease about the conditions of these workers and was left wondering what life was really like in that mine.

In Durban, if we were ever inclined to forget it, two small incidents would bring home to us aspects of the *apartheit* system. The first happened when I decided to take a bus in the town and went to stand at a bus stop. Three white men came hurrying out of three nearby shops and warned me that I was standing at the *nie blankes* bus stop and must move forward to the right bus stop for me. I had not thought of separate bus stops; of course, I moved. In the circumstances prevailing at that time the men were being helpful.

A few days later, while we were still in Durban, our car was broken into in the hotel's car park and some small items stolen. The police had a suspect and I, as the owner and driver of the car, was summoned to court to identify myself. When I was called to the witness-box, I rose and took my place in what looked to me like the witness-box. For a moment, there was a flurry of concern in the court—this time, I had gone into the *nie blankes* witness-box. I had to climb two or three more steps to another witness-box, for whites. Certainly I was unobservant but I wonder how many people unfamiliar with the system would have thought of looking for different witness boxes. Such arrangements are surely history now in the new South Africa; I merely relate my own experiences in 1960.

There was another unfortunate experience when we had left Durban and taken the famously lovely Garden Route south along the coast towards Cape Town. At East London we were motoring one evening after dark with a local friend. She was driving a brand new MG car of which she was very proud. As we were cruising along at about forty miles an hour, a large object loomed up in front of us and there was not enough time to stop before we collided with it. The object turned out to be an ox, which did a kind of handstand over the bonnet, or hood, of the car. The car was badly dented, though still roadworthy. The ox appeared to walk away into the darkness none the worse for wear.

There was a regulation in force at the time that if cattle were moved on the roads at night they must be preceded by someone carrying a light. Our friend knew this and as there had been no light she wanted to report the accident to safeguard the no-claims bonus on her insurance. The police were called and everyone waited for an officer to come. While we waited, the owner of the cattle, a white farmer, came to the scene and there was some discussion between him and our friend. Eventually a white police officer arrived, accompanied by a black constable. The accident was duly reported and as we left we could see the police officer in conversation with the owner of the cattle.

Penny and I had to leave East London before the case came up in court. We all thought it would be straightforward and that our friend would have no difficulty in proving her point. It was not so. When we reached Cape Town we heard that, in court and under oath, the police officer had testified that unfortunately the owner of the cattle could not be traced. As eyewitnesses we might perhaps have been helpful but of course it was too late. We wondered what must have been the thoughts of the constable, who had seen and heard it all.

Cape Town

If the drive towards Johannesburg had impressed us with its natural beauty, nothing had prepared us for the magnificence of Cape Town and its environs. First, as we approached the city with the open sea to our left, we could see and admire the beautiful vineyards on the hills to our right, and the whitewashed, traditional Dutch farmhouses. Then there was the almost Mediterranean atmosphere and character of the town itself, with the seaport so close that one could disembark from an oceangoing liner and walk straight into its streets. And to the west, the narrow Cape Peninsula curved away into the distance, all blue and as if floating in the sunlight; Robben Island, now world-famous as the place where Nelson Mandela and others would be incarcerated for so many years, was somewhere there had we known it. We took the cable car to the top of Table Mountain and gazed at the panorama and the town spread out below us, admiring the splendor of the scene and happy, now, to have arrived here at the end of our journey.

When our week in Cape Town ended, our ships were due to leave within a few hours of each other on the same day. Penny would go east on her way back to Mombasa; I would go west on my way to Southampton, England. We watched the car dangling from a crane as it was taken on board the Holland Afrika Line ship on which I would be traveling, and felt it looked very small and brave to have rendered us such faithful service down the length of half a very large continent.

Postscript

In Salisbury, I did see again the friend from London whom I had met on my last evening in Nairobi. We had dinner and, afterwards, spent many hours together, talking late into the night. We had many interests in common and quickly seemed to become very close. He spoke of all the interesting things we would do together when I reached England, all the places we would visit and all the interesting people we would meet, and there were weeks for it all to take root. I always knew he was married and when I said so, he said, yes, but they no longer lived together—and I believed him because I so much wanted to! To me it was a sort of wonder. I would find a letter from him, he said, in Johannesburg. No letter came. Perhaps it would be in Durban? I could not believe that something that had seemed so real was not. I told myself there must be a reason, some explanation.

Penny had her own, sensible doubts about the relationship from the beginning. She just did not believe that in the real world things happened like that. Although I tried to conceal the strength of my feelings, she could not be unaware of the tension they caused in me and while on the surface we continued as before, our previously easy companionship was affected.

When at last we met again in London, he took me home to meet his wife, with whom he was living, and my weeks of illusion collapsed very painfully. Nothing was said. I spent a wretched night in their spare room and left in the morning to carry on with my life.

It was a complicated situation in many ways. A message he sent later through a mutual friend to say that he had been sincere came too late to be much help. By then I had anyway collected my wits and embarked on a challenging new endeavor.

Chapter Five

Back in England, 1960–'72

In October 1960, when the ship docked in the port of Southampton, my parents were there to welcome me. They had left Nigeria during the previous year owing to my father's ill health. The doctors in London had found that he had contracted numerous strains of malaria—more, apparently, than they had ever previously encountered in a single patient. By the time I reached England, he had recovered his health and, at the age of fifty-seven, had pursued with characteristic determination a course in accountancy, despite having no natural liking for work with figures. Now he was commuting by train to London daily from a new home in Sussex, having secured a post as accountant at a voluntary organization, the British Diabetic Association.

We cleared the customs with some difficulty, since the officer I approached appeared to have negative feelings towards a person coming on a ship from South Africa. The car seemed eventually to pass muster, but then he spotted my watch and demanded to know when it had been bought. I said about five months ago in Nairobi, and that it had been worn by me ever since. "Ah!" he said, "It's less than six months old!" whereupon he pocketed on behalf of Her Majesty's government the sum of five pounds as import duty. He then told me that if I had anything else dutiable in my baggage, it was in his power to confiscate everything I had brought with me! I had a meerschaum pipe I had brought for my father from Tanganyika but luckily forgot it in the hour of need and was able to assure him with sufficient conviction that I had nothing else to declare, so with apparent reluctance he let us go on our way.

A few months later, on returning from a trip to France, another customs officer asked about the same watch, and I produced my receipt for the duty already paid. This officer scrutinized the receipt for a moment, then remarked that sadly his colleague in Southampton who had issued it had been killed in an accident two months later. As he said this he raised his eyebrows and gave me a slightly quizzical look, from which I gathered that his colleague might perhaps have been known within the customs service for giving some passengers a hard time. While doing his duty that officer had certainly given me an uncomfortable reception on my return to the home country after four years away.

First Mention of Cobham Hall

A few months' paid leave that were still in hand were mostly spent with my parents or visiting friends and relatives, generally picking up the threads of life in England. Then one morning my father returned briefly to the house after leaving for his office to bring me a copy of the *Times Educational Supplement*, a weekly publication indispensable to the world of education in Britain. On the front page of this particular edition was a photograph of Cobham Hall, a large, historic country house in the county of Kent, in southeast England. The caption under the photograph stated that a new independent, international and interdenominational secondary school for girls, with a special interest in world affairs, was to be founded there. There was a short piece on an inside page, which mentioned the names of one or two people involved in the project but not much more.

I showed the paper to my mother, commenting that this was what I would like to do. She looked at the photograph and caption and said, "Yes, dear, I think you would like teaching there."

"Oh no," I said. "I'd want to be the head of it!"

"Oh!" she said. "Well, you could always *try*."

And we both laughed. At that point I had no way of contacting anyone concerned with the project so there was nothing much I could do about it.

That New Year I started working as assistant to the Student Affairs Officer of the United States Information Service, which was then housed at the north end of the American Embassy in London's Grosvenor Square. I took a room in a mews cottage within walking distance of the embassy and for several months found this new job to be an interesting and congenial occupation. The work focused mainly on encouraging good relations with the many African students in London, and it seemed to provide a bridge between the time I had spent in Africa and a resumption of interest in the issues and preoccupations then prevailing in the West.

Joining in January 1961, my arrival at the embassy coincided with President John F. Kennedy's "Hundred Days." Very impressive policy papers flowed through the office, setting out ideas on many and diverse topics with a vision sometimes reaching towards the end of the century, well beyond the more familiar political focus on the next election. The president himself visited while I was there, and the entire staff of the embassy was invited to be addressed by him.

His easy charm and charisma were very evident at that meeting and I believe he made everyone present feel cheerful and rather proud.

Cobham Hall Reappears

It was part of my job to scan four daily newspapers, the *New York Times*, *Washington Post*, *London Times*, and *Guardian*. One day during the summer, I was looking at the *London Times*, which was still in its old, traditional format with columns of short notices on the front page. As I turned over the page another advertisement leapt out at me like a frog leaping out of a pond. They were looking for a Head for the new school to be opened in autumn 1962, at Cobham Hall.

By coincidence, a friend from Kenya whom I had met two or three times since we had both returned to England, on that same day chose to visit me in my office for the first and only time. I showed her the advertisement, and she immediately insisted that I must apply. I had forgotten that I had mentioned Cobham to her at all, but she said I had talked about it every time we had met! Well, I could *try*, couldn't I? Taking some leave that was due to me, I carefully put together a letter of application and sent it off.

There followed a long, informal meeting-cum-interview at her home with one of the founding governors most closely involved in the project, Mrs. Ann Money-Coutts, then further meetings with others similarly involved. It was clear that a great deal of work had yet to be done if the plan for the school was to materialize but a Board of Governors was beginning to take shape and Mrs. Bee Mansell, later designated the Founder of the school, was a driving force full of conviction and enthusiasm.

I much later learned that there had been another prospective head appointed at the time when, towards the end of 1960, I had first seen the photograph and brief report about the school. She had withdrawn from the undertaking and the recent advertisement had produced applications from several older candidates well into their fifties, and from me. I was not yet quite thirty, but I believe the originating governors thought a younger head might be more suitable for their purposes than an older one; they offered me the job with a retainer pending further progress. I told my American boss at the embassy what was afoot and soon was free to take up the new work.

When I was applying for the job at Cobham Hall, and before meeting any of the people involved, I paused to ask myself whether I really wanted, should I be successful, to bury myself in an unknown boarding school tucked away somewhere in the countryside. I decided that, yes, I probably did. My attitude at the time was that if one wanted to do something constructive for the future, it would have to be in either politics or education. I had no experience or contacts that might lead into politics, so for me it must be education. Where and how were "in the lap of the gods." What had attracted me to Cobham from the start was the brief outline I saw of the school's proposed character and ideals, with which I was wholly in sympathy.

When, having been interviewed and offered the job, I first went to see Cobham Hall I was stunned. I had seen that early press photograph of part of the house but beyond that I had no knowledge of the house or its setting. Seeing Cobham Hall itself was a revelation; it looked to me like a kind of lesser version of Hampton Court. The Gilt Hall alone was amazing with its Inigo Jones ceiling, ornate stucco and marble walls, Snetzler organ and exquisitely inlaid floor. This lovely, great house, set in potentially beautiful though then largely neglected grounds and surrounded by countryside, yet only twenty-five miles from London, was no obscure setting for a school. It was far more than I had expected and the possibilities were obvious. From then on, I was ready to take any risk and weather any storm to hold on to the opportunity the Cobham project offered.

The Preliminaries

There followed weeks and months of intense activity, mostly directed at securing financial support. New governors were recruited and periodic board meetings were held which I attended, though never as a member. A trust was formed, which for no particular reason that I know was called the Westwood Educational Trust. Articles of Association were drawn up to which I was asked to contribute the paragraphs dealing with the aims of the school (what an opportunity!); and detailed planning started about how the interior of the house could be adapted for its new purpose.

It soon became clear to me that while the originators of the project were wholeheartedly committed to promoting it, others on the Board who were also acting as advisers were equally though not so openly committed to saving them from their folly. Certainly it is the duty of responsible advisers to steer the people they are advising away from unacceptable risks and I am sure that was what these advisers were doing. However there was more to it than that, for at least one of them expressed to me in an unguarded moment that he had a strong, personal distaste for some of Mrs. Mansell's cherished ideas, in particular that the school should be interdenominational in character. By dint of sustained effort and persuasion, however, the required sum of risk capital was raised, the last contribution coming from a supportive governor during the weekend before a deadline set for the following Monday.

The decision was therefore taken to proceed and a Press Conference was called to announce the project and hear me address the media as prospective head. This took place at Chatham House in London on February 7, 1962. The whole event was arranged and orchestrated by Frederic Doerflinger, a senior executive at the London offices of the large American public relations firm then known as BBDO; he and his English wife were early friends and backers of the school, and subsequently sent their daughter, Alice, there as a pupil. The resultant press coverage was astonishing; Fred eventually produced a record of it all in a binder, one or two copies of which may possibly have survived in the archives at Cobham Hall. A friend in Kenya wrote and told me that a report had even appeared on the front page of the *East African Standard*.

It was also through Fred Doerflinger's help that a *Sunday Times* magazine included Cobham Hall in a two-page spread listing the leading public (i.e., private) schools for girls in the country. The column dealing with waiting lists for entry in the following September stated that in the case of Cobham, unlike most of the rest, places were still available since the school was only due to open then. The heads of the other schools listed, all of them well-known establishments, were possibly not best pleased to see an as yet nonexistent school listed among their number. Nevertheless, it was a very helpful achievement on Fred's part, since at least a quarter of the founder pupils at Cobham were attracted to the school by that one piece of publicity.

There is, no doubt, often an element of serendipity in setting up any new project. There is a story about a long-time governor of Cobham Hall, Richard Page-Croft, a maltster by profession from Ware in Hertfordshire. Mr. Page-Croft used in the early 1960s to give an open invitation for luncheon on Mondays to all his friends to join him at a restaurant just off Regent Street in London. In that busy restaurant, to which Mrs. Mansell had taken me one Monday to meet Mr. Page-Croft, we were seated at a long table, just a little way along on the opposite side from our host. Bee was discussing the need to increase the representation of financiers from the City of London on her newly forming Board of Governors, in order to strengthen its credibility when raising capital for the school.

There were in the City then two influential and well-known men who happened to have the same last name; one's first name was Ian and the other's was Hugh. People were saying they thought Ian would be an excellent choice but Mr. Page-Croft thought he was probably too busy to take the project on. So I looked at him and said, "Would Hugh do it?"

"Me?" he said. "I had never even thought of it!"

Twenty-four hours later, he rang Mrs. Mansell to tell her that he would be very happy to join her Board of Governors and for some twenty-five years, until soon before his death, he was a keen and faithful governor of Cobham Hall, always amiable and well-liked by girls and staff—and all as a result of a mishearing in a crowded restaurant. His daughter Miriam became a pupil at the school for several years and used to recount with an amused smile how proudly her father would talk at home about his school.

A Difficult Birth

The press announcement that the school would open in the autumn notwithstanding, it soon became clear that the battle was far from over. It was as if nothing significant had changed; the board remained paralyzed with dissension. While I was busy in London dealing with a flood of correspondence and meeting parents interested in sending their daughters to the new school, and doing my best also to find qualified teachers willing to risk their careers on this new and untried venture, the truth was that absolutely nothing was being done to set in motion the essential work of preparing the beautiful but old and partly derelict building in Kent to receive its first intake of pupils and staff. The only work then being done was that commissioned by the national Historic Buildings Council, which had undertaken to hand over Cobham Hall in a wind- and weather-proof condition at a favorable price provided it was opened to the public on twenty-four days a year. Some three, critical months passed in this way.

During that time, successive board meetings continued to be held at the lawyers' offices, all ending inconclusively. Eventually matters came to a head. I was to attend yet another such meeting in early May and woke up on the morning of the meeting with an unmistakable inner instruction to agree to defer the opening of the school until January 1963. All over the country, then as now, the school year started in September. I had been insisting for weeks, if not months, that such a course would be fatal to the project—now I would have to concede. Slowly, I got ready and left for the lawyers' City of London offices. Arriving after the meeting had started, I was met as I emerged from the elevator by a distraught but usually supportive governor with the words: "Brenda, *can't* you say that the school can open in January?"

I went into the room, took my seat and when the question was put to me again said yes, I supposed it could. The opposition was jubilant and suddenly full of bonhomie; Bee Mansell broke down in tears and asked me if I had gone mad; everyone else was, I think, exhausted and possibly somewhat bemused by the turn of events. The meeting broke up almost at once and I made my way back to the apartment I was sharing near Selfridge's in Oxford Street, wondering what could possibly happen now.

What happened was twofold. First, the steam was let out of the boiling pot, so to speak, which then lost the momentum to regain the same intensity. Secondly, a 'white knight' turned up and took the whole project in hand with immense energy and determination, so that the school opened on schedule, in September 1962. However, more of that later.

Kurt Hahn

Soon after my appointment as prospective head of Cobham Hall, I was introduced by an early governor of the proposed school and personal friend of Mrs. Mansell to the eminent pioneer educator, Kurt Hahn, founder of Salem School in Southern Germany. After Salem School was infiltrated by the *Hitlerjugend*, Kurt Hahn had left Germany and gone to Scotland where, in 1934, he founded Gordonstoun School, famous among other things for its 'Outward Bound' ethos of fitness, self-reliance, enterprise, and meaningful service to the community.

When I met him on that occasion in the autumn of 1961, Kurt Hahn asked me to take over the girls' house at Salem School, which had reverted to its original purpose after the end of World War II. I doubted that my German was fluent enough but said I would think about it, though only, of course, if the plans for Cobham Hall did not materialize. He, having decided what he wanted to happen, was not a man to listen with much attention to such a response and I was later told that from then on he considered that I had let him down!

When the British press covered the story about the opening of Cobham Hall, several articles for some reason dubbed it "the girls' Gordonstoun". Gordonstoun, now coeducational, was then a boys' school and there was no conscious imitation intended by us. However, of the three titles we chose to use instead of the traditional ones for school officeholders two were, without anyone at Cobham knowing it at the time, also used at Gordonstoun. Our 'Head Girl' was known as the Guardian, and she was elected and not, as was usual in England, appointed. Perhaps the education journalists were right even then in perceiving some kind of affinity between us.

Briefly to run ahead of the story, several masters who had taught at Gordonstoun went on to be heads of schools themselves, carrying with them the Kurt Hahn ethos. They formed an international association of like-minded schools which they called 'The Round Square Conference' (named, I believe, after a building at Gordonstoun). At the outset, all the schools in membership were boys' schools. Two of them were Box Hill School in Surrey and Aiglon College near Montreux, in Switzerland.

In 1970–'71, there were various comings and goings between Cobham and Box Hill, as a result of which the then head of Box Hill, Roy McCormick, one day brought John Corlette, the head of Aiglon College, to visit Cobham. Out of this came an invitation for me to attend as an observer a gathering of the Round Square Conference headmasters at Aiglon in summer 1971. After that meeting, the headmasters decided to break from their established practice and bring Cobham, a girls' school, into membership, and the suspected link with the Kurt Hahn philosophy manifested itself again and became from then on an acknowledged part of Cobham Hall's purpose and character.

How the School Came to Be Started

As already stated, the original moving spirit behind the project to start a new independent school for girls in 1962 was Mrs. Bee Mansell. As Miss Bee Batlivala, she had been the first Indian woman to qualify as a barrister at the Inns of Court in London. She subsequently became for a time Director of Education in the Indian State of Baroda, now part of Gujarat. She then married an Englishman, Guy Mansell, and they settled in the southern English county of Sussex with their only child, Edwina.

Bee Mansell had been educated at the prestigious Cheltenham Ladies College, a large English private school for girls, in the days of the famous Lilian Faithfull as Head. By 1961, Cheltenham had a different head. Having regaled all her friends and dinner guests for several years with the exceptional merits of Cheltenham, Bee decided when Edwina reached the age of seven that she must be taken to see the school and meet the current head. It so happened that the latter, when offered the opportunity to meet Edwina, suggested that such a meeting would be more appropriate in a few years' time. Bee was deeply hurt; Miss Faithfull would have been so happy, she thought, to meet her former pupil's daughter. After that incident, she fell silent on the subject of Cheltenham.

Then one evening, when Bee was wondering about a suitable school for Edwina, one of her dinner guests asked her why she did not start a school herself. Bee leapt at the idea. She embarked on the project with great determination and energy, scouring the newspapers for likely large houses and persuading and cajoling support and promises of financial contributions from all her wide acquaintance. To emphasize the international nature of the school she had in mind, she secured her friend, Mrs. Vijaya Lakshmi Pandit, sister of Indian Prime Minister Jawarhalal Nehru, as a Patron of the future school.

At first, Bee was interested in Hinchingbrooke House, a large, old country house in what is now Cambridgeshire, which had just come onto the market; but that was then for lease, not for sale. Reluctantly, Bee abandoned the idea of Hinchingbrooke and just then Cobham Hall was advertised, for sale, to be used for local government offices, as a large company's training establishment—or for a school. Bee moved fast and secured first-refusal rights. It was then that the saga of forming a Board of Governors, forming a Trust and raising the necessary capital had begun in earnest.

When Mrs. Mansell was negotiating for the purchase by the Trust of Cobham Hall, she had the benefit of knowing what had happened to another relatively new school, Cranborne Chase, when it had had to move to new premises in New Wardour Castle. That school, now closed, had accepted a government grant for the work needed to make the building sound; the actual cost of the work had far exceeded the amount of the grant and the generous help of a wealthy patron had been needed to keep the school solvent. Bee therefore negotiated not for a fixed grant but for Cobham Hall to be handed over already wind-and-weather-proof, while accepting the Historic Building Council's conditions about the opening of the house to the public and other conditions relating to, for example, insurance. As a result, the extensive repairs needed to the fabric of Cobham Hall, such as reroofing, including that of the leaded towers, rebuilding the beautiful, Elizabethan brick twisted chimneys, preserving and restoring the ceilings of the Gilt Hall and the State Bedrooms, plus the removal and making good of certain structures affected by dry rot, were done at the expense of the Historic Buildings Council.

White Knight

After the seemingly catastrophic Board meeting in May 1962, at which the decision was taken to postpone the school's opening until January 1963, news of this development reached Mr. Anthony Stephens, of the Baltic Exchange in the City of London. Mr. Stephens had recently stepped in to rescue a small private school near his home in Surrey. He was a large man with a large personality, who enjoyed this role and delighted in getting things moving, being fully prepared to 'knock heads together' if necessary in order to do so. Anthony Stephens saw with great clarity the impending disaster and the very public embarrassment the Governors' divisions and indecision were about to cause. I believe he did his own research into each individual's financial position, after which he called them all to his house. I was not required to attend; I heard later that he had been making enquiries about me with Miss Stott at the Kenya High School.

According to the version that reached me afterwards, at that meeting Anthony Stephens spelt out their situation to the governors with his characteristic forcefulness, stipulated how much personal investment would be required from each, secured their undertakings, became a governor himself and personally undertook the huge task of preparing Cobham Hall in the few months remaining for its first term, beginning in September 1962. This development must have come as nothing less than a godsend to Mrs. Mansell and her friends on the Board; it certainly did to me. I had done nothing yet to reverse my own work of the preceding months, which was all therefore still in place so that none of this now needed to be known by those, mostly parents and girls—including several from overseas—who would have been affected.

Getting On with It at Last

Anthony Stephens strove mightily to get Cobham Hall ready in time. The ongoing work on behalf of the Historic Buildings Council was essential, but it would not provide heating, lighting, modern kitchens—all the necessary infrastructure for a school. Central heating alone for that big, old building was a daunting project, especially in the short time available. The only organization willing to undertake the task at such short notice was one called the Coal Utilization Council, so the school started with coal-fired heating.

From late June until September 1962, a small team of dedicated workers from that Council lived on site in a caravan in the old walled garden at Cobham and hammered away seven days a week, digging up flagstones and floorboards, installing hundreds of yards of piping and innumerable radiators, building the necessary self-feed burners and their housing and, somehow, got the bulk of the work done in time.

Before opening day our first Bursar, a retired rear-admiral submarines, warned me repeatedly with much foreboding that Cobham with its old walls, many of them three feet thick, would take weeks to warm up. In the event, to my surprise as well as his, everything worked beautifully and the parts of the building we were going to use first were comfortably warm within twenty-four hours. That happened barely a week before the first girls arrived. The sinks in the kitchen were being installed during the morning of the day of their arrival.

The supply of hot water for the newly installed bathrooms, being dependent on progress with the heating system generally, caused much anxiety up to the last few days. Anthony Stephens speculated cheerfully about bringing steam engines into the East Court of Cobham Hall to supply hot water if all else failed. It did not come to that, but at times it looked as if it might.

Meanwhile, work had to proceed also on rewiring, decorating, equipping; even dual purpose tennis courts/netball pitches were laid in the old walled garden ready for the first term. The school's first deputy head, Beryl Green, spent much of this time at Cobham assisting Anthony Stephens and also choosing and ordering desks, chairs, chalkboards, stationery, textbooks, and much else that would be needed. I was still mostly in London doing my best to make sure, among other things, that there would be girls and staff to use all this, immediately and in the future.

The bedrooms at Cobham were furnished almost entirely with a bulk purchase from an establishment in London for foreign students, which just happened to close and sell up its contents during that summer. For years, Cobham Hall girls would hang their clothes on hangers marked Bridge House.

There had been prolonged and heavy rain during the English summer of 1961, which had greatly aggravated the damage to many parts of the building. In particular, it had saturated a heavy oak beam above the ornate, Inigo Jones ceiling of the Gilt Hall to which was attached a large chandelier. Now sodden, this beam was in danger of putting pressure on the ceiling. One of the most impressive and delicate achievements of the restoration workers was the way in which they carefully removed the old oak beams above the Gilt Hall and replaced them with rolled steel joists, then pinned up from above the ornate ceiling inch by inch. I found it reassuring to know that the heavy old chandelier in the Gilt Hall was suspended from a stout RSJ, when later so many people were sitting or standing below it.

Although warm, lit and plumbed, the house was constantly covered with dust both before and after the school opened. Apart from all the restoration work with its generous contribution of dust, large areas of the old floors had had to be sanded. During the first year, 1962–'3, every girl had a blue duster, hastily purchased for us by a founder pupil's mother, tucked into her waistband so that she could use it to clear the dust from any surface before she sat or leant on it. Anthony Stephens and one of the brave originating governors, Lady Virginia Ogilvy, later Lady Airlie, worked hard one Sunday afternoon before the girls arrived in an attempt to quell the clouds of dust in a long upstairs corridor. Ginnie swept vigorously with a scarf tied round her head as protection from the dust and Anthony Stephens worked so energetically that day that his belt broke and he had to knot his tie round his middle to replace it.

Many people made at some point a vital contribution to the beginnings of the school at Cobham Hall, but none did so more indispensably during those months of preparation than Anthony Stephens. He was like a man inspired and he appeared to enjoy every moment of it.

Early Days at the School

The school started with just over fifty girls aged between eleven and sixteen, five teaching staff, a qualified nurse, and an almost miraculously helpful maintenance man who, sadly for us, left at the end of the first year taking with him as his wife the school's excellent and irrepressible Spanish cook. Only two wings of the H-shaped house and the central block were in use at the outset, others being restored and opened in succeeding years as numbers grew.

Even after some parts of the building were occupied, in others restoration work of many kinds continued. This meant in practice the constant presence of teams of workers from a large and well-known construction company. Some of the men carried on quietly with their skilled work for the Historic Buildings Council, while others doing regular construction work for the school were fond of loud whistling and, of course, chatting with the girls whenever possible. It was reassuring and much quieter when a successful local builder took over all construction work at the school. His was a smaller, family-run business and from the day his workforce came on site they never caused a moment's noise or disturbance.

A frequent visitor to Cobham Hall during its earliest days was a personage then known as one of Her Majesty's Inspectors of Schools, Miss Margaret Rees. As a new school we had to wait for two years, undergoing regular supervision and informal inspection, before a full inspection would be carried out and the school could be officially recognized as efficient. This was important to us because when the recognition came it made recruitment of well-qualified teaching staff easier. Miss Rees, a small, dignified, astute and very helpful person, became during those years a familiar figure at Cobham—so much so that she featured in one of the girls' end-of-term skits inspecting, as I recall, a Speech and Drama class during which the girls were all lying flat on their backs on the floor of the Gilt Hall being trained in the art of relaxation.

Ron Billings

Ron Billings, the above-mentioned local builder, came to Cobham Hall first as a father interested in sending one of his daughters to the school as a day student. He started our conversation by making it clear that there was no way he would be willing to be involved in any construction work at Cobham. We then went on to discuss his daughter's education. Before he left, I took the opportunity just to share with him the ground plans our architect had drawn up for a new tuition block. He was immediately interested. He disapproved of the plan for the roof, which he said was fashionable at the time but would cause all sorts of problems later. He thought the estimates were excessive and, frankly, that he could do a better job for much less—and all his reservations were forgotten.

The Historic Buildings Council's work was by then at an end. Some governors were at first reluctant to change companies but were persuaded by the obvious economic and other advantages on offer and Ron Billings took over all construction work at the school. He started, of course, with the new tuition block, and I soon came to appreciate his verve and efficiency. It was Ron's idea that the corridor and classrooms of the new building should be carpeted, which greatly reduced their potential for clatter and echo.

It was Ron Billings too who made it possible for Cobham Hall to have a good swimming pool. After the school had run a successful garden fete in summer 1964 specifically to raise funds for a pool and raised the then princely sum of £2,000, Ron offered to build at his own expense a good-sized pool, covered and heated for year-round use, provided the other parents agreed to a termly contribution (I remember it as £6) until the cost, fixed by this generous action and therefore not subject to inflation, was paid off.

Yet another of Ron's contributions during my time at Cobham was the creation at our request of a crèche for the young children of teaching and other staff. This was probably one of the first crèches, if not the first, provided at such a school in Britain. We satisfied all the relevant regulations and specifications at the time but these have now snowballed to the point where such an enterprise might not be feasible. The idea of providing a crèche was prompted by the wish to keep good staff we knew and liked during the sellers' market for teachers, which prevailed in the United Kingdom in the 1960s. The visible and audible presence of young children on the premises was anyway a welcome facet of life at the school.

The Ron Billings I knew had the characteristics of a benevolent, energetic and very enterprising patriarch. Once he decided Cobham Hall would be good for his family, his interest in the school never waned. He went on to construct much else at Cobham, including a purpose-built house providing study bedrooms for the senior girls, which was ceremonially opened by Margaret Thatcher in 1971 when she was Secretary of State for Education. Ron continued to be a great friend and help to the school long after my own days at Cobham. It was a very lucky day for us when he decided to send his daughters and granddaughter to Cobham Hall.

Bowing Out

My own involvement with the Cobham project lasted just over ten years. After our touch-and-go beginnings the school grew steadily; and by the time I left it was at full capacity with 280 girls, about 40 of them day girls, and some 26 teaching staff, including part-timers. As already indicated, we had outgrown the accommodation provided by the house and new, purpose-built structures had gone up.

One could probably write at length about the rest of those ten years but any such stories might come best from former students and others involved in the school's development. Certainly there were ups and downs, real triumphs and, thankfully, no real disasters. Seeds of animosity sown by all the conflict and angst before the school began lingered for many years among a minority of habitually absentee governors. Happily, those memories were eventually laid to rest when the late Caroline Cawston, a one-time pupil known by all at Cobham as Corky, was voted in by a later governing body as its chairman. Competent and successful in running her own business, Corky not only knew how to safeguard the school's financial interests in critical times but also, having herself been one of its earliest pupils, understood its spirit and knew what went on—which almost as much as anything is what one hopes for in a chair of governors.

By the time I handed over to my successor, I felt that many of our stated aims and ideals had been accomplished, some wholly, some in part—but by no means all. One aim high on my own list had been (of course) to keep the atmosphere as positive and *happy* as possible. Teaching groups were kept small—from the beginning we used, advisedly, the word 'group' instead of the more usual class or form. Unlike the general practice at the time, little stress was laid on competitiveness in the academic sphere, which with good teaching the ablest did not need but could be unnecessarily discouraging for others. It is often argued that competitiveness is essential to inspire motivation but this policy proved capable of producing some remarkably satisfactory results. Intense competitiveness was reserved for group activities such as inter-House competitions in sports, music and drama, which are, basically, fun.

One dream which I was briefly able to realize at Cobham, important to me at the time but with particular significance to me later on, was the creation of a 'Silence Room' near the top of one of the towers. I believed there should be a place set apart for the use of anyone who wanted to escape the noise and bustle of life in a boarding school and just be quiet. The Silence Room was also partly inspired by the installation by Dag Hammarskjold, as Secretary

General of the United Nations, of a Meditation Room at the United Nations Headquarters in New York. The focal point in the Silence Room at Cobham when I was there was a painting in oils of a serene and beautiful Head of the Christ by the Italian American sculptor, Joseph Nicolosi. The Silence Room was never to my knowledge used by many girls but it was used by some, and it was there.

For me the Cobham years had been absorbing, creative, multi-faceted, filled with loving humor. Certainly there were the unrelenting routine demands of my role, but much fulfillment too—as well as moments of profound frustration. The lives of the children of fee-paying parents are not necessarily more plain-sailing than anyone else's and, just as in any school, one is concerned with the welfare of a community of human individuals.

When I left the school, however, I left. It would not have been right or necessary to interfere with the work of my successors and anyway I needed to move on. The Cobham episode had been an absorbing focus while it lasted and to break with it was hard. What I did not know was that by relinquishing it I was being freed for something of transcendent value that would profoundly affect the rest of my life.

A view of Cobham Hall in Spring.

The Gilt Hall at
Cobham Hall.

The author at
Cobham Hall.

PART II: AFTER

CHAPTER SIX

Next Steps

Before leaving Cobham Hall I had felt exhausted and was in no hurry to seek new employment. A generous check from Cobham parents as part of a leaving gift encouraged some traveling. Having received a warm invitation to visit the family of our one Peruvian girl I was thinking of spending a few days with them in Lima before going on to see the Inca ruins at Cuzco and Machu Picchu. What stopped me was an uneasy feeling that I could go to Peru and come back from Peru—but nothing would have changed.

I started to feel instead that any traveling I did must take me to India. Without knowing what I was looking for I knew I was looking for something, or someone. To give my journey an external purpose, I put together the outlines of a world tour that would include visits to centers for refugee children, and went to see the leading personnel of non-governmental organizations active in that field. Visits were suggested to the Tibetan Children's Homes in Mussoorie, North India, and children's homes in Saigon and Macao. Afterwards,

I might attend a Round Square conference in San Francisco, visit a cousin in Mexico City and return to England via Bermuda where a founder member of the teaching staff at Cobham Hall was living, married to a diplomat. In the end I got no further than India and stayed there for several months.

The only place on the wish list where I had nowhere to go and knew no one was Delhi. A friend at London University had given me an introduction to a woman he knew who was working for the British Council there. Just before I left England my mother also gave me a letter she had received after contacting a speaker whose talk had impressed her. This provided two pages of advice about how to meet Tibetan spiritual leaders while in Delhi and ended with a postscript, which suggested seeking out an Englishwoman, Mrs. Pamela Knight, who had a home in Delhi and would surely help.

Delhi—Mrs. Knight

Arriving in Delhi in March 1972, I checked in at a hotel for a night and in the morning contacted the British Council officer to whom I had been given the introduction. She readily offered her house as a base during my stay. Since she would be at work all day, she encouraged me to feel free to come and go as I pleased and was welcoming and helpful, as was her elderly Muslim house servant.

Discovering that Mrs. Knight's address was within walking distance I went to see her as soon as possible. Luckily she was at home in Delhi, for I came to know later that she had other homes in other countries. A gracious, elderly woman, she received me warmly even though, again, I came as a total stranger. There were many items of Tibetan art in her home, and colorful handmade Tibetan rugs on all the floors. When I arrived the door was opened by a young Tibetan woman.

In response to my enquiries, Mrs. Knight told me that there were three spiritual personalities who were held in high esteem by people in north India at that time. One was a woman Saint, known as Anandamayi-ma; Mrs. Knight showed me her picture but said she was living away from Delhi, so that it would be difficult to meet her. She then showed me a painting of someone she called "our Baba", saying he was silent and explaining that he, too, was not easy to meet since he was then living in Simla. Finally, she showed a photograph of Dadaji, who was in Delhi and easy to visit. Dadaji was previously known as Dr. D. J. Mehta, and had been Mahatma Gandhi's medical doctor. Mrs. Knight told me that, after Gandhiji's assassination, Dadaji "had taken to the spiritual life" and was running an organization known as the Society of the Servants of God. Mrs. Knight offered to take me to see Dadaji the following day.

Dadaji's premises were in a part of Delhi called Chanakyapuri, near many of the foreign embassies in the city. As soon as Mrs. Knight introduced me to him, Dadaji asked me if I had come to see him as a tourist and I assured him that no, I genuinely wanted to learn from him. He then invited me to sit on the floor like several others in the room, a chair was found for Mrs. Knight, and the discussion that had been under way was resumed.

Mussoorie

After that first meeting with Dadaji I took a bus from Old Delhi to Mussoorie, a hill station to the north of Delhi, to spend a few days with Mrs. Taring who was in charge there of a large establishment for orphaned Tibetan children. She too was kind and welcoming. I had read about Tibetan Buddhism and besides seeing the orphanage I was keen to meet other Tibetans who had taken refuge in Mussoorie, and to see their new and ornate temple. I was touched by the gentleness and plight of the Tibetans I met but discovered that, face to face with the outer mode of expression of Tibetan Buddhism, I could be no more than an interested and respectful observer. This reinforced in me a growing sense of inner void. Religions were interesting but insufficient; an absorbing job, which had also been home, had been relinquished; idealism to achieve had burnt low: there was a *void.* I knew that only something very real would help.

On my way back to Delhi, I stopped for dinner and to spend the night at the invitation of Mrs. Vijaya Lakshmi Pandit, whose home was near the bottom of the hill below Mussoorie. As already mentioned, Mrs. Pandit, well known in the West as an eminent diplomat, was from before its inception a Patron of the school at Cobham Hall; I had later come to know that she was also a personal friend of my father's eldest sister, my Aunt Irene. Mrs. Pandit welcomed me very graciously. She was keen that I should meet her daughter, the well-known novelist Nayantara Sahgal, and asked me to contact her when I reached Delhi, which, of course, I said I would be happy to do.

At Dadaji's

On my return to Delhi, Mrs. Knight told me that Dadaji would meet with me alone and in the event we spent about three hours together. Understandably he assumed that I, only recently arrived in India, knew nothing about Indian thought and philosophy, with the result that although I could not have claimed to be at all learned in such matters I found that mostly he was introducing me to much with which I had long been familiar. While I was grateful for Dadaji's kindness and the time he gave me, this too was not for me. I would be drawn to someone who *knew* what I knew! As I took an auto-rickshaw back to the house of my friend, the warm March wind blowing through my hair, I remember thinking that while this was disappointing I would much rather settle for nothing than deceive myself. I would visit Dharamsala, and then continue my journey as planned.

Dadaji was scheduled to hold a public meeting the following Thursday evening to mark *Ramnavami*, the birthday of Sri Rama, the great God-man celebrated in the epic known as the *Ramayana* and much revered by Hindus in India. Feeling that I must pay my respects to Dadaji before moving on, I decided to attend that meeting. In the meantime, I went with a tourist group by train from Delhi to Agra to see the Taj Mahal, which exceeded even my highest expectations. The majestic prospect as you approach it and the astonishing beauty and intricacy of the inlaid stonework seen close-up were like nothing I could ever have imagined. If nothing else had come of my visit to India, just seeing the Taj might have been enough.

There were already many people assembled in the large hall when I arrived for Dadaji's meeting and, spotting Mrs. Knight among them, I went across the hall to join her. She welcomed me kindly and asked how I had been getting on since we had last met, then said, "Our Baba is here today", indicating Baba who was quietly sitting cross-legged at the front of the hall next to Dadaji.

My first impression of Baba was that I had never seen such striking eyes. I wished at once and many times during the ensuing talks that I could meet him. Dadaji spoke at some length after which a short message from Baba was read out, since Baba did not speak and was not accompanied on that day by a companion who usually interpreted his hand signals. Baba's message was in poetic language: "My life is like a dewdrop on a perfect bloom; it is the teardrop shed by the Angel of Silence. To adorn beauty, I borrow a ray of light and behold eternal mystery for a moment." (For the full text, see appendix 2 on page 207) There was total silence in the hall while Baba's message was read.

At the end of the formal proceedings I made my way through the crowd to where Dadaji was sitting, made my *pranams*, i.e., bowed low to him with joined palms. He pretended gently to cuff my ear, whereupon I smiled and he smilingly patted the other ear. I was happy to be assured of his understanding. I then went back to stand by Mrs. Knight, who seemed to know almost everyone in the hall. Soon she asked me if I would like her to introduce me to Baba and of course I responded with an emphatic "Oh yes, please!"

I Meet Baba

We went over to where Baba was sitting and after greeting him fondly Mrs. Knight introduced me: "Baba, this is Brenda, from England, who would like to meet you." I, very conscious suddenly of being large, hot and western, did my best to bow down and greet Baba suitably. Baba gave a slow and rather imperial nod and that, it seemed, was that. Mrs. Knight and I returned to where we had been standing previously.

When Baba walked up to us and wrote on a pad of paper he was carrying "You can come and see me on Saturday at eleven" I saw the message at once and turning to Mrs. Knight told her Baba was addressing her. Baba shook his head and nodded towards me. Me!—Baba was addressing me? Then I was fumbling again: I had remembered that I had arranged to visit Ms. Sahgal on that Saturday morning at 11.30. I told Baba this, feeling anxious lest some other time might not be convenient. He indicated that it was no problem and wrote, "Then come at 2.00." In writing, Baba asked Mrs. Knight to help me to find my way and all was settled.

CHAPTER SEVEN

Baba Takes Over

Baba was staying with a general and his wife in Army quarters in Delhi. On Saturday afternoon, after a friendly and interesting meeting with Ms. Sahgal in the morning, I was conveyed by Mrs. Knight's driver in her car to the general's house where I was made welcome and taken to see Baba in his room.

Baba first asked me to read out to him from a printed booklet his last speech on Silence given the day before he had made his vow of lifelong silence ten years previously, in February 1962. This is given in full in appendix 1. After I had done so I found I was telling Baba all that had been happening in my life as if I had known him forever. Throughout this first meeting Baba was holding and handling a beautiful, stylized figurine of Christ, about eight to ten inches in length. In India, Baba is an affectionate term meaning father, or it may be used for a baby son or some other much-loved family member. The term is also commonly used for a person believed to be of spiritual standing. As most of us know or have heard, there are innumerable babas, saints and *sadhus* in India; the hope or challenge is to approach one who is real.

Savithri, Baba's lifelong companion, would not arrive in Delhi from Simla until the following day so mostly Baba just listened, though from time to time he would write something on his pad for me to read. I told Baba about my plans for a world tour. He wrote that they would not help me, what I needed at that juncture was rest and so much traveling would merely add to my exhaustion. That made sense to me. I had always thought I was reasonably independent but dropped the idea of the tour then and there. With this Baba, such a reaction came to me naturally, effortlessly.

It so happened that this meeting with Baba took place on the day on which I had been given an open invitation to accompany several other westerners, who were going to join the crowds at a very large open-air meeting in Delhi at four o'clock that afternoon to be addressed by another, very different baba, known as Satya Sai Baba. On the plane coming to Delhi, several young people sitting near me had been talking enthusiastically and at length about Satya Sai Baba and telling me that I must be sure to go to see him. By four o'clock that afternoon, I had lost interest in going to see any other baba. I was with Baba until quite late in the evening.

For one more night I returned to the house of my British Council friend. Next day, when Savithri had arrived, Baba arranged for me to stay with him during the days and to spend the nights at the house of good friends who lived nearby, since Army regulations did not permit a foreigner to stay overnight in a general's house. I had already been nearly three weeks, on and off, with my first hostess who had so generously allowed someone she had never met before to use her home.

In 1972, when I first met Baba and Savithri, both were in their early forties. Baba wanted Savithri and me to be good friends and he played a little trick on her. Baba's host, General Mohinder Singh, was a robust man, over six feet tall, who, with his turban, seemed even taller. Baba told Savithri about me and said I was as big and tall as Mohinderji and Savithri was therefore expecting to meet some kind of female giant. The result was that when she saw me her first comment was, "Baba, she's not *so* big!" Savithri herself was a graceful, elegant woman of slight build. We became lifelong friends.

One of the first things I came to know about Baba was that he could indeed know anything without your having to tell him. Naturally, that seldom deterred people from telling him what was on their minds. Baba took an early opportunity to show me that he knew what I was thinking. On the Sunday, he was seated on a sofa in the living room with a group of people sitting on the carpeted floor in front of him. I was sitting at the back of the group and Savithri was sitting beside Baba, "reading" his hands; Baba used a system of hand signals of his own devising which, with a practiced interpreter, enabled him to communicate in English with surprising speed and eloquence.

This being 1972 when the youth drug culture was in full swing, particularly in the United States, there were many Western hippies wandering around India and the discussion turned on the advantages and disadvantages of what was going on. I had just been reading Charles Reich's book *The Greening of America,* and was thinking about it. Baba suddenly looked straight at me and started to refer to this book while Savithri, reading Baba's hands, hesitated over the word, greening. Remembering the thoughts I had had on leaving Dadaji the previous week I was happy to receive Baba's message.

Kurukshetra

The following day I had planned to go to Dharamsala where the Dalai Lama had his headquarters. Baba suggested that instead I should accompany him and Savithri on a visit to Kurukshetra, about sixty miles north of Delhi. There, a project was under way to build an enormous 'tank', in this case more like a very large lake or reservoir in which at least one hundred thousand people a day could take a ritual bath and pray. In fact at the time of a solar eclipse in July 2009, more than a million people were reported to have converged on the great tank at Kurukshetra for the ritual bath and prayer.

Kurukshetra is a sacred place, since it was the site of the battle which is the central event of the great Indian epic, the *Mahabharata*. It was on the battlefield of Kurukshetra that Lord Krishna gave to the warrior, Arjuna, the teachings recorded in what is believed by many people to be one of the finest of all scriptures, the *Bhagavad Gita*. Baba, whose full title is Mouni Baba (*Mouni* meaning "silent"), was the moving spirit behind the creation of the great tank at Kurukshetra. The government of India, fronted by the Home Minister of the time, Gulzarilal Nandaji, and with the full support of the Prime Minister, Indira Gandhi, took on the implementation of this historic project. I was told that the Hindu community also donated almost unlimited private funds. The tank is surrounded by steps and elegant pavilions in red granite. It is one mile by two miles in dimension and is reputed to be one of the landmarks visible from outer space. Three rivers were diverted to supply the water for the tank.

Baba, Savithri and I were driven to Kurukshetra by car. When we arrived, Gulzarilal Nandaji—he was almost always referred to with the honorific suffix -*ji*—was already at the site waiting for Baba. This visit gave me an early opportunity to witness the respect with which Baba was treated in India by some of the highest in the land.

Gulzarilal Nandaji was by some thirty years Baba's senior in age, yet he treated Baba with respect amounting to reverence, was always very humble in his presence and openly called Baba his *guru*. He was three times acting Prime Minister of India, an immensely powerful figure in the government and the Congress Party, and could have been the President of India had he so chosen. Honored just before the end of his life with the *Bharat Ratna*, India's highest civilian award, Nandaji was one of the outstanding, first-generation leaders of independent India, a man in the Gandhian mold, who lived simply and took almost no salary for any of the important posts he held. He was totally incorruptible. He lived to the age of one hundred years, as Baba had once told him that he would.

Baba had come to attend a meeting that day with Nandaji and Bansi Lal, who was then Chief Minister of the State of Haryana in which Kurukshetra is situated and subsequently became the Union Defense Minister. The meeting took place in a guesthouse that was part of the project. At one point, Bansi Lal was tempted to play the Hindu card and boasted that he would not allow Muslims to rise in his State. I then saw for the first time the fiery side of Baba's nature. Speaking of course through Savithri, Baba objected furiously to Bansi Lal's statement, telling him that he had put Bansi Lal into his position as Chief Minister and could as easily remove him from it if he wanted to abuse his power by being unfair. Bansi Lal, in front of all his staff, immediately apologized and touched Baba's feet.

After the meeting, we went with Baba to visit a model dairy that was part of the overall project at Kurukshetra. Baba gave each of the cows from his own hand a big lump of *jaggery*, a delicious, unrefined sugar that cows—and most humans—greatly enjoy. Cows are loved and respected in India for their gentle nature and their generosity in giving their milk for the benefit of humans. It is partly for this that they are held by many to be sacred.

This first visit to Kurukshetra was for me an absorbingly interesting experience and an eye-opener, which strengthened the feelings I had spontaneously formed for Baba two days earlier.

Baba and Savithri stayed in Delhi for a few more days. After that, it was time for Savithri to return to her post as an Economic Research Officer at the Labour Bureau in Simla, an offshoot of the Ministry of Labour in Delhi. Savithri, I came to know later, was an academic gold medalist with an advanced degree in Economics from the University of Madras. While we remained in Delhi I spent almost the whole of every day with Baba, just being included in whatever was going on. There were several visits with people who were anxious to see Baba again, having been close to him when he and Savithri had been living in Delhi before they moved to Simla.

One outing took us a little beyond the city to a plant nursery specializing in *bonsai* cultivation. Baba had heard me express a wish to see the Qtub Minar, one of the sights of Delhi, and on our way back he stopped all the cars—there were several with us that day—and everyone visited the Qtub Minar. Sightseeing being, as I realized later, normally no part of Baba's program, this was a kind gesture towards a newcomer, which clearly not only I but all enjoyed.

To Simla and Rock House

When they returned to Simla, Baba and Savithri took me with them. We went by train from Delhi to Kalka, the nearest Indian Railways station to Simla. There is a narrow-gauge mountain railway from Kalka to Simla, but we went up the steep climb to the hill station by car. Simla, now Shimla, is built high on the side of one of the foothills leading to the Himalayas. On a clear day one can see the mountains in the distance. It had been the summer seat of the pre-Independence British government in India.

Baba's home in Simla was Rock House, which has historic associations with the Freedom Movement since it was where Jawaharlal Nehru had lived whenever he had come to Simla. A few hundred yards up the road from Rock House was Viceregal Lodge, the summer home of the erstwhile Viceroy; by 1972 this had become the premises of the Indian Institute of Advanced Studies. In design and setting it is reminiscent of some grand country house that one might see in England as a legacy of the Victorian era.

This first visit to Simla consisted of three wonderful weeks at Rock House. During the day, while Savithri was at work, Baba would often sit with me at one end of a long, heavy table in a large room that served as both dining room and kitchen, and he would write what he wanted to say on his notepad. We would discuss many things. It was Baba's custom when a discussion ended to tear up the sheets of paper on which he had written. This was when the scene described at the beginning of this memoir took place, when Baba wrote that he knew everything and I had found being with him so uniquely reassuring.

The headquarters of the Western Command of the Indian Army was in Simla. Baba had many friends among the senior officers living there with their families, and quite often in the evenings we would all go and visit them in their homes. Savithri told me that at that time Baba was affectionately known as "The Baba of the Western Command". During this visit Baba, Savithri, and I went one day to a studio for a photograph of the three of us together, as if to mark a reunion.

When people first come into what one might call Baba's orbit, the impact can be very powerful. One unforgettable moment came when, in Rock House, I woke up in the morning with a sudden glimpse of a time, in another life, of great intensity. I dissolved into uncontrollable tears. Baba called me over to where he was, put his arm round me and said through Savithri, "Why do you cry now, when you have Baba forever?" For me, that was a life-changing experience.

Baba's first visit to the United States, via Canada, had been in 1971. After those first three weeks spent in Simla he was going to leave for England, after which he would again visit Canada and the United States. Baba wanted me to stay with Savithri until we could both join him in England and accompany him and Rosa, a friend living in England, on a tour of several European countries before leaving for Canada.

We returned with Baba to Delhi and very soon were at the airport seeing him off. Many people came with garlands for Baba, there was bustle and activity, and suddenly he was gone. It was a painful parting even though we knew it would not be for long. Savithri and I went back with General Mohinder Singh and his wife, whom we knew as Deedi, to their home. I then spent one more night with our friends along the way and next day we two took the train back to Kalka and returned to our empty home in Rock House.

Baba at the Kurukshetra tank, c.1973.

Baba with
Gulzarilal Nandaji
at Kurukshetra

Baba and Savithri
with the author,
Simla, 1972.

CHAPTER EIGHT

With Savithri in Simla

Mouni Baba's apartment was on the top floor of Rock House. It consisted of two large rooms and a bathroom. One room was used as a bedroom /sitting room and the other room, with the large table, was the dining room, one end of which was used for cooking. Near one wall of the bedroom was an almost life-sized image of Sai Baba of Shirdi, the first spiritual Master in Baba's line, and a number of other photographs and pictures including Baba's self-portrait in oils, which is reproduced on page 193.

The bedroom had a window with a deep recess big enough to seat two people. The window was protected by a fine wire-mesh screen to restrain, not mosquitoes, but monkeys, which abounded in Simla and used to enter houses and shops whenever they could to snatch food or whatever took their fancy. There was a beautiful view from the window, though not of the mountains since the room faced south. Also in this room was a handsome wooden box containing velvet-bound copies in English of the *Guru Granth Sahib*, the sacred scripture of the Sikhs. While Savithri was at the office, I spent many hours reading these, starting with the Introduction, which gave the history of the ten Sikh *Gurus*.

Savithri's office was a short walk away from Rock House. During the week I was on my own and could take the rest that Baba had prescribed. It was a very hot summer that year, which must have been terrible in the plains. While I was in Simla with Savithri, the town became for a while very full and busy with a Peace Conference following the border dispute of the previous year between India and Pakistan. This culminated in the Simla Accord, which remains the basis for the 'line of control' between the two nations in Kashmir. Prime Minister Zulfikar Ali Bhutto, accompanied by his daughter, Benazir, attended the conference for Pakistan, and Indira Gandhi attended as Prime Minister of India.

In the evenings when Savithri was free we would go to visit friends or take a walk in the cool of the nearby woods, ending with a delicious glass of hot, sweet tea seasoned with cardamom and made over an open fire in a tiny, makeshift tea shop not far from home. At weekends, we would do our grocery shopping at the vegetable market and at a long-established business called Spencer's, where you could find almost anything; then treat ourselves to a meal out.

Parampara

The time I spent with Savithri in Simla was a gentle learning time, during which I had ample leisure for reading, and also absorbed from Savithri herself many things about her life with Baba and its background. She familiarized me with the term, *parampara:* a Sanskrit word meaning the unbroken line of succession of a number of spiritual Masters (usually male though, rarely, in a female body). In India there have been many such lines of succession; one example is the line of the ten Sikh *gurus*, the centuries-old line of Shankaracharya is another.

Christianity has presented Jesus down the centuries not only as a supremely great and adorable incarnation of spiritual power, love and beauty, but also as uniquely and forever the *one and only, ever,* incarnated Son of God. This has been divisive and has, no doubt, also helped to make many people in the west, and most churchgoers worldwide, unreceptive to the notion of there being God-realized spiritual Masters present on earth at all times, whether openly or in seclusion.

The *parampara* is important because the relationship between *sadguru* and *shishya*, i.e., between Master and chosen successor, offers authenticity. If people do not know this, or forget it, they may be deceived. It can also happen that, out of rivalry or insufficient under-standing, other people around a Master find it next to impossible to accept his choice. This would not affect the truth, which is that the chosen successor will be led by the Master to a level of awareness in which he knows he is a God-realized being just as surely—as Meher Baba puts it in his book *Discourses*[3]—as an ordinary person knows himself to be a human being and not an animal.

As already mentioned, the first spiritual Master in Baba's line was Sai Baba of Shirdi. Sai Baba's chosen spiritual successor was known as Upasini Maharaj, or Upasini Baba. Upasini Baba chose a woman, Godavari Mataji, to succeed him in running his *ashram* in Sakori, which is about three miles from Shirdi in the State of Maharashtra; and it was Upasini Baba who was responsible for bringing Meher Baba back to normal consciousness of the material world, after he had been awoken in Poona to his divine status and mission by a kiss

3.   Meher Baba, *Discourses*, Sheriar Press, seventh revised edition, 1987, page 277.

from a Perfect Master[4] known as Hazrat Babajan. Meher Baba was Mouni Baba's spiritual Master. These specifics I gradually came to know as I spent time with Baba and Savithri and then alone with Savithri. They came as no surprise; I had read enough and heard enough and thought enough, for long enough, to be aware that such people existed.

Brief Note on the Three Previous Masters

The great Sai Baba of Shirdi, who as a very old man left his body in 1918, is today worshipped by millions of people in all parts of India. Increasingly people from other countries also revere him but in India his well-known image, sitting on a rock in a torn robe and with his right ankle resting on his left knee is to be seen everywhere— in homes, shops, taxis and in the auto rickshaws, the three-wheeler conveyances that are to be seen on the roads everywhere in India; it makes no difference whether you are in Shimla in the north, in Kerala in the south or in places in between. Hundreds of millions of people are devoted to Sai Baba and about a hundred thousand daily make their way to Shirdi to visit his tomb. All are welcomed and fed. The Sai Baba Trust, now run by the government of the State of Maharashtra, employs some three thousand people to receive the devotees.

During his lifetime, it is said that Muslims thought Sai Baba was a Muslim and that Hindus thought he was a Hindu. He needed no such label; it was too evident that he loved everyone and every living creature. Even now, if you go to Sai Baba's tomb in Shirdi no one asks you who you are, where you come from or to what religion,

---

4.   'Perfect Master' or, in the present context, 'Master', is used as an English translation of the Sanskrit term, *sadguru,* meaning a fully enlightened or God-realized *guru.* Baba once said that even a great Saint is as a candle to the true *sadguru's* Sun.

if any, you belong; it would all be irrelevant. It is a fact of history that man-made religious constructs have divided people and caused innumerable deaths all over the world. Sai Baba's most powerful message was that *every* human being belongs to him.

One can find references to Sai Baba of Shirdi in sourcebooks, and on the internet, but relatively little has been printed about him. I read one slim volume, *The Incredible Sai Baba*[5] by Arthur Osborne while I was in Simla in 1972. However, so many people believe in Sai Baba and still experience his help in their lives that there can be few in the Sub-Continent who do not know who Sai Baba of Shirdi is.

A disciple is trained by his *guru* in the way that is unique to the individual. *Upasana* means intense spiritual discipline. Upasini Baba was given that name by Sai Baba after he had accomplished what to most of us would be an unimaginable feat: he sat alone in rapt contemplation on a hill near Nasik for one full year *without food or drink*—yet lived.

A Master chooses his outer mode of expression according to his destined role in the world. Upasini Baba's outer mode of expression was characteristically Hindu. For thousands of years there had been no place for women in the Hindu religious life. Upasini Baba not only trained a woman as the future head of his *ashram* in Sakori, he also lived openly as a naked *fakir* and picked forty young women to be as his daughters, who were very well educated in Sanskrit to understand the sacred scriptures of India. It was a groundbreaking innovation and a symbolic forerunner, perhaps, of the almost worldwide changes that have been taking place during the past century in the status of women. Upasini Baba left his body in 1946.

---

5.   Osborne, Arthur, *The Incredible Sai Baba, The Life and Miracles of a Modern Day Saint*, first published 1958; several subsequent editions available.

Meher Baba was born in 1894 to Parsee, or Persian, parents in Poona (now Pune) in India. He led a normal life as a schoolboy and at college until the age of twenty, which was when he was awakened to his spiritual status by that kiss from a *sadguru* in a female body, Hazrat Babajan. After two more years he went to Sai Baba in Shirdi seeking help; Sai Baba sent him to Upasini Baba. He was with Upasini Baba in Sakori for seven years before he branched out as a Baba in his own right.

Meher Baba's chosen mode of expression was totally different from that of his *guru*. He traveled widely in India and in the West, visiting England, Europe, the United States and Australia, and published a number of books in English containing unique insights into spiritual matters and the meaning and purpose of life; many of these have been translated into other languages. He neither sought nor avoided the press attention and publicity that came his way and was utterly indifferent to whatever people chose to say or write about him. He repeatedly said that he had come "not to teach, but to awaken". New teachings were not required, mankind had been given the truth by the Great Teachers of the past and what was needed now was to live that truth. He himself worked indefatigably with children, poor people, mad people and the God-intoxicated (known as *masts*), seeking out masts all over India in order to help each one in his own way[6]. From 1925 until he left his body in 1969, Meher Baba kept silence. "If my Silence cannot be heard, of what avail words?" he once responded to a questioner while visiting the West.

---

6.   For Meher Baba's work with masts, see William Donkin, *The Wayfarers*, Sheriar Press.

Sai Baba of Shirdi.

DON'T WORRY –
BE HAPPY.
    —Meher Baba

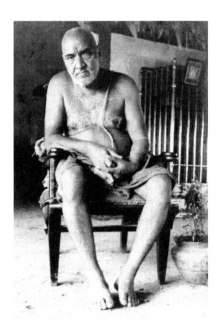

Upasini Baba

Santaji

To return to my stay in Simla with Savithri, we were fortunate that during the months we spent there together Sant Gulab Singh, generally known as Santaji, was also at his summer residence in Simla. Santaji was already then in his nineties. I was told that, as a young man, he had been a lawyer. Once, his turn came to defend a man whom he knew to be guilty of a serious crime. An inner voice told him not to do it but he thought he was imagining things and carried on. Three times this happened, and after the third warning he suddenly became almost completely deaf and had to tell the court that he could not continue. He turned his life around and became a very much loved and respected Saint among his fellow Sikhs and also the wider community in India and abroad.

Santaji always received Savithri and me with great kindness and affection. We used to sit with others in his house or outside under the pine trees, listening to his talks or his readings. I felt that I had some personal link with him from the past and he once asked me, "Do you really not remember *anything*?" And dumb westerner that I am I had to admit that I did not! In Santaji's garden were some enormous magnolia trees covered in blossoms and he would allow us to take some home, since he and we knew Baba was particularly fond of magnolias.

Mikhail Naimy

As already mentioned, while we were in Simla on our own Savithri told me many things about her life there with Baba. One memorable event she told me about was the arrival in Simla of Mikhail Naimy, the well-known Lebanese author and friend of Khalil Gibran. Mikhail Naimy had come at the invitation of the then President of India, Dr. Radhakrishnan, to inaugurate the Indian Institute of Advanced

Studies. Baba and Savithri had made a point of going to the Institute to meet him.

Mikhail Naimy's best-known work in English is *The Book of Mirdad*,[7] a work of great wisdom and beauty. The fictional Mirdad kept silence for seven years before breaking it to electrify his companions with his teachings; he was particularly eloquent on the subject of silence. When Baba and Savithri met the author they had felt an immediate affinity, and subsequently exchanged some memorable correspondence: "Of the innumerable faces my eyes came across during my short stay in India," wrote Naimy in a letter to Baba, "yours and your sister's (Savithri's) haunt me the most and I am very pleased to have them about me."

Khan Saheb

Another treasured friendship Savithri described was with Vilayat Khan, revered as an *Ustad*, or master, of the sitar, who was also then living in Simla with his wife, Monisha, and their son and two daughters. They had a beautiful, old-style house called *Pari Mahal* (Fairy Castle) situated just above the main town, where six or seven students learning the sitar under Khan Saheb were housed in a separate wing. At Monisha's invitation Baba and Savithri had visited *Pari Mahal* and the whole family had become friends.

Vilayat Khan had a very big music room, which he treated almost as one would a temple. In this room he kept instruments that had been with his family since the time of his distant forbear, the fabled singer Tansen, who had performed before Akbar the Great in the sixteenth century. Next door, Vilayat Khan had his practice

7. Naimy, Mikhail, *The Book of Mirdad*, written in English and first published in Lebanon by Sader's Library in 1948. Many subsequent editions published. Watkins Publishing edition, 2011.

room. Savithri told me that for a public performance he would have several accompanists; however when he played in his practice room just for Baba, he would be accompanied by a single *tabla*-player. The playing would start at about midnight, after a leisurely dinner enlivened by the wit of Khan Saheb who was also a talented raconteur. The midnight performances would last for several hours, creating an atmosphere of almost magical intensity. Vilayat Khan's son, Shujaat, is also internationally known as a master of the sitar.

Ramzan

Another friendship Savithri told me about was with Ramzan, a Kashmiri railway porter who had become a friend from the day Baba and Savithri had arrived in Simla. Ramzan often came to dinner at Rock House and Baba and Savithri would sometimes go to eat at his home, usually after visiting the cinema. Once Baba took Ramzan with him to Delhi and showed him the Red Fort and other famous sights of the capital. When Ramzan had made a short visit to Kashmir to be married, Savithri told me that Baba had had an entire bridegroom's outfit made for him in raw silk, which he gave to Ramzan already packed in a suitcase ready for the journey.

Savithri recalled that on one occasion when there had been a particularly heavy fall of snow, Ramzan had come to Rock House and knocked at Baba's door late at night. In normal weather, it was at least half an hour's walk from Ramzan's home to Rock House. When Savithri answered his knock at the door, Ramzan had told her that he could not sleep for thinking of Baba on the top floor of Rock House in such a heavy fall of snow. After Baba and Savithri finally left Simla, Ramzan returned to Kashmir and they lost trace of him.

Enter Scott and Heidi

There was a story too about the arrival in Rock House of Scott and Heidi, two young Americans from Minnesota. Several friends were sitting around Baba one afternoon when he suddenly asked one of them to hurry down to the road below and bring to him two young westerners whom he would find there. He ran downstairs and soon saw the two young people, who looked to him rather like hippies. He approached them, greeted them and said, "Baba is asking you to come and see him."

Scott, whose hair was kept fashionably long, responded, "I'm not interested in seeing any barber!" "No, no" the other explained, "Not barber, Baba. You really must come and meet Baba." With this clarification, the two were quite willing to be conducted to a meeting with Baba. They were almost penniless and by this time their health had begun to suffer from their wanderings. Baba took them under his wing, keeping them with him in Rock House each day and giving them the benefit of his superb cooking for a few weeks. He then sent them by train to Kerala, where they were cared for and lived as family with Baba's parents for more than a year.

Scott and Heidi's role in this phase of Baba's life has special significance for it was Heidi's parents, Ken and Betty Haan, who first invited Baba to visit Minnesota, where from 1971 Baba mostly spent the greater part of each year. Their youngest daughter, Wendy, also became close to Baba and for several years accompanied him and acted as his main interpreter in the United States.

We Leave for Kerala

Savithri and I were meant to stay in Simla for two months, after which Savithri would apply for several months' unpaid leave. The plan, as we know, was for us first to visit for a month Baba's parents and his Shrine of Silence in Kerala, in the south, and then fly to England to join Baba and Rosa, the friend with whom Baba was staying, for a month touring France, Germany, Switzerland and Italy.

Savithri having been, if anything, underemployed at the Labour Bureau for the first two months we spent in Simla together, discovered when she applied for leave that her bosses found her to be indispensable. They produced a research project for her to design, a task which would take at least a month, and our departure from Simla had to be deferred. Eventually General Mohinder Singh, who was on the point of retiring from the Army, came to Simla on Army business, heard what was going on and intervened. This enabled us to leave after only one extra month, but as a result we missed the tour with Baba and Rosa in Europe.

The rains had started by the time we left, and the journey by taxi down from Simla to Kalka was slow and hazardous for the road was severely affected and at places there were large boulders to be negotiated. Then, having arrived in Kalka, we sat and roasted in the Delhi train for an uncomfortably long time until the train left the station and the fans came on. We spent barely a day in Delhi before continuing our journey via Madras (Chennai) to Cheruvathur, the small town near Baba's parents' home and estate in north Kerala. The train journey from Delhi took two days.

Prasanth and Baba's Parents

All the many westerners who, over the years, visited Baba's home in Kerala and were looked after by his parents knew them only as Amma and Appa, which of course means Mother and Father. Appa was a quiet, small, wiry man, gentle and kind in his ways but always very much in command of everything at Prasanth, which is the name of the property and means a Place of Peace. Amma was voluble, witty, warmly caring of everyone and a wonderful cook. In 1972 both were getting on in years but still very active.

Amma was married at thirteen and waited many years before Baba, her first child, was born. During those years, she and Appa were living in Ooty (Ootacamund) and looked after forty orphans, providing for all their needs. Appa was, with his brothers, then in the wholesale fruit and vegetable business. Amma wrote articles on feminist subjects for publication in the local press—this was in the 1920s; she once told Mahatma Gandhi, who was visiting her father's house in Cannanore (Kannur), that if the Freedom Movement did not win freedom also for women, she would not be interested in it. A second child, a daughter, Lalitha, was born when Baba was nine years old, at about which time Appa gave away four-fifths of his fortune to his brothers and the family moved to Prasanth. Both parents eventually lived into their nineties.

Baba's parents were devout and very knowledgeable about the Sanskrit scriptures; they were close to Narayana Guru, the great philosopher-saint of Kerala who died in 1928 and who was instrumental among other things in breaking the grip of the caste system there. There is in Prasanth now a photograph showing Appa and Savithri's father and others with Narayana Guru; Baba's and Savithri's families were friends all their lives.

Everyone whom Baba sent to Prasanth was made welcome by his parents. Young couples came from the United States and brought their children and they would all be lovingly treated as family. It was a lifestyle of unusual selflessness and hospitality. Savithri and I had a very happy visit with Amma and Appa; I remember Amma telling joke after joke at the dining table, all of course in Malayalam, the language of Kerala; Savithri was laughing so much that she was unable to share the jokes with me and I just laughed along with everyone else and enjoyed the fun.

Baba had been keen to send us to Prasanth before we left India, in part because he wanted me to see his Shrine of Silence, which I now attempt to describe.

The Shrine of Silence

Baba's Shrine of Silence is carved out of a single, huge volcanic rock, about two hundred yards from the house at Prasanth. There was a small, natural cave in the rock, which was extended to over a hundred feet in depth in order to create the shrine. When I first went to Prasanth, there was a painted sign by the path: *Shantidham*, which also means Place of Peace, or Stillness.

To enter the shrine is like walking into a rare and beautiful sculpture. There are no straight lines, and every contour was carefully designed and carved by hand—no power tools were used—in 1970 by Baba, with the help of a young Englishman with a doctorate in nuclear chemistry, Christopher Guzy. Some fifty others also worked on the site and the exterior landscaping. The shrine took a year to complete. Baba said he had carried the dream of the Cave-Shrine for twenty-five years before he was able to bring it into being.

There are three chambers; the floor of the first has been covered in 'Black Galaxy', a black granite with flecks of gold in it. The entire interior of the shrine was originally lined with a cream-colored marble mixture suggestive of alabaster. Now the walls have been painted but the floor of the two inner chambers remains unchanged. There are three steps down to the middle chamber, which leads by a gentle slope to the innermost chamber. There is a single electric bulb hidden at eye level on the furthest wall behind a carved, circular rosewood frame with a 280-carat golden topaz set in its center. When the doors and windows are closed and the gem is in place, the only lighting in the shrine consists of shafts of iridescent color coming through the topaz.

There are no images in the shrine. There is no talking, no music, no reading—just silence and stillness. The Shrine of Silence is designed as a beautiful space where anyone, from any religious background or none, can bow to God in his or her own way in silence, without need of an intermediary. Many people sense a very powerful Presence there.

When the work on the Kurukshetra tank was almost completed Gulzarilal Nandaji came to Prasanth and lived for a week in silence in Baba's shrine. Over the years others have followed, for quite long periods or short. Many people come to Prasanth just because they have heard about Mouni Baba's Cave-Shrine and wish to see it. Although Prasanth remains a home and is not a public *ashram*, whenever possible all are made welcome.

More About Prasanth in 1972

When Savithri and I were at Prasanth in 1972, Amma had an old-fashioned Kerala kitchen in the house where the cooking was done on open wood fires. The way things were done at Prasanth at that time reflected elements of a traditional way of life which went back some ten thousand years, but which is now rapidly disappearing. Amma's kitchen was her domain, where fresh coconuts from the estate were grated, and wonderfully tasty food was prepared in the Kerala style. Good Kerala food is not typically as heavily spiced as in some parts of India further north; partly thanks to the liberal use of coconut it is relatively mild, yet full of flavor. At Prasanth there are many jackfruit trees, mangoes, custard apples, cashews, coconut palms, pepper vines, in fact, all kinds of tropical fruits and vegetables. American visitors sometimes say it reminds them of Hawaii.

Baba in his Shrine of Silence at Prasanth

CHAPTER NINE

We Leave for England, Canada, and the United States

After a month with Amma and Appa, Savithri and I left via Mangalore by air for Bombay, now Mumbai. General Mohinder Singh and Deedi were by then already living in Bombay, the general having retired from the Army and taken up a post with the Tata Company. They received us at the airport and we spent one night with them in their new home before flying on via Delhi to London. Baba had already left England for Toronto.

We had three or four days in England before leaving again to join Baba in Toronto. After a short stay with Baba and friends there we flew on with Baba to our final destination, the "Twin Cities" of Minneapolis and St. Paul, in Minnesota, USA. This was Baba's second visit to Minnesota and there was quite a large welcoming party at the airport to receive him. Soon we were all driven to Green Lake, near a very small township known as Chisago City, some thirty miles north of the cities. A lakeside cottage there was to be Baba's main base for the next three months.

Green Lake

This was a beautiful location. The cottage was the last building near the end of a small peninsula. There was a landing stage on the lake in front of the cottage, a raft anchored a few yards further out for diving or sunbathing while the Minnesota weather permitted, a pleasant lawn and plenty of space for children to play. All this provided a perfect setting for Baba's purposes at the time, for throughout the duration of our stay at Green Lake numerous people came, as in the previous year, to spend time with him. Most but not all were young, often young couples who brought their small children. There was rarely a day during those three months when fewer than thirty would be there for the midday meal and/or dinner. Baba who, like Amma, liked to cook and did it superbly, took charge of preparing most of the meals and everyone helped with the rest of the work.

In 1972 there was, perhaps, an even more clearly marked divide than usual between the youth culture and the attitudes of the majority of their elders. Many of the young people who then flocked to meet Baba kept their hair long, dressed very informally and many talked openly of using psychedelic drugs. Baba never approved of the use of such drugs and worked in his own way to help all who were affected by them. He represented something different and much more genuinely inspiring.

One young woman, never a hippie, who had heard about Baba from Heidi and had written to Baba even before she met him, was Renée Reed. Renée had come to see Baba on his first day in Minnesota in 1971. Baba advised her then to stay with him, but at the time, she had an independent life which she was not yet ready to abandon. Five years later, she came to be with Baba. She dedicated her life to Baba and was the main US interpreter of his sign language for at least thirty years. She is by profession a librarian. From a leading family in the black community in St. Paul, she attended the prestigious Carleton College in Northfield, Minnesota, spending a year in England as part of her course, and did her Master's in librarianship at Rutgers University. From 1973 to 1976 Renée worked at Harvard University in the Widener Library, and subsequently at the Radcliffe College Library. After she returned to Minnesota to be with Baba Renée held a succession of posts in Twin Cities libraries and later joined the Hennepin County Center for Innovation and Excellence, charged with working for improvement across all aspects of the county's departments.

Ruby Cup International Inc.

In the early 1970s, the exchange control regulations for Indian citizens traveling abroad other than on business were draconian— Indians were only officially permitted by the Indian government to take with them the sum of $8. This meant that unless one had a sponsor or came on business, one had either to start some sort of organization and seek charitable funds (as many have done) or to come as someone's guest. Even if there are willing hosts the latter cannot be acceptable if one means to visit often and at length; as for charity, Baba never sought or accepted any in his life, nor would he ever start or join any organization.

There is, however, no natural law that spiritual Enlightenment must be accompanied by unworldly incompetence. In 1973 Baba started, with the help and support of three families who had become close to him, a company known as Ruby Cup International Inc. This dealt mainly in the export from India and import to the United States of handmade carpets. The company continued in business for several years; at one time there was a 'Ruby Cup International' shop in Minneapolis and a 'Baba's Shop' in Rochester, Minnesota, the home of the Minnesota Mayo Clinic. An important objective of the Ruby Cup company was to provide useful experience and employment for several young people whom Baba was keen to help. The latter included two of Baba's stepsons from a marriage of seven years' duration, which he contracted with Isabelle Thorson, of Blooming Prairie, Minnesota. Isabelle's terminally ill husband had begged Baba to look after his wife and their five young adult children after he was gone.

There exists a real ruby cup. It is a small, short-stemmed goblet rather like a loving cup, shaped for Baba over three years by a gem cutter to resemble a lotus flower, with petals inlaid with gold and the map of India inlaid with gold on the interior of the cup. The cup in its finished form weighs 660 carats and is unique. Baba's gemological expertise was particularly well known and very highly respected in many parts of India.

CHAPTER TEN

Back in England:
Picking Up the Threads

After almost a year away, it was time for me to return to England and think about what to do next. While in Simla I had been in correspondence with James Douglas, the director of the Conservative Party's Research Department, which then had its premises in Old Queen Street next to St. James's Park in London and near the Houses of Parliament. The daughters of some members of Parliament and ministers of the time were students at Cobham Hall and the idea of applying for a post at the Research Department had come from the Right Hon. Anthony Barber MP, later Lord Barber, who was then the Chancellor of the Exchequer. Mr. Douglas had invited me to contact him on my return to England; now I did so, and was asked to go to see him.

A Taste of Westminster Politics

This led to a job as a Research Officer in the Social Affairs Section of the Department, starting in mid-January 1973. My first assignment was to brief Conservative members of Parliament about housing policy; as may be imagined, this necessitated some very rapid learning on my part.

Research probably was not the right word for the Research Department. It was more a question of information collection for the purposes of policy formulation, support and presentation, culminating among other things in the production of the Party's Manifesto[8]. The research department was also seen by many as a kind of training ground or incubator for aspiring parliamentarians. Before long, I too started applying for selection as prospective parliamentary candidate for various constituencies in and around London.

Having missed out in Putney, then my local constituency, which went to David Mellor MP, I was selected for Lambeth Norwood, also in south London, where there was a Labour Party incumbent, John Fraser MP, later Lord Fraser. The boundaries of the Norwood constituency had recently been redrawn to include parts of Brixton, not known as propitious territory for a Tory, or Conservative, candidate. I was that candidate for Norwood in each of the two 1974 General Elections that led to Labour victories and, despite lively campaigning and the efforts of an energetic band of helpers, in both we lost. I only hoped that some of the many children from the Lambeth council estates who joyfully ran off with blue "Vote for Brenda" stickers on their lapels did not meet with too warm a reception when they reached home.

---

8.   In this quite substantial document, a political party sets out its plans and intentions for the five years following a general election, should it be elected.

I found it interesting that Conservative and Labour campaigners seemed to understand each other well, so that when our paths crossed there was no particular display of rancor. It was the local Young Liberals who became loud and vituperative if they saw me. I suspect too that they were the ones who pelted our campaign wagon with rotten tomatoes in Brixton; luckily I saw them coming and closed the window in time. Even a lone, self-proclaimed member of the Communist Party, who regularly came to our sparsely attended campaign meetings, would only afterwards shake his head and pay me the dubious compliment of murmuring that, come The Revolution, he doubted if they would bother to hang me. But back then those particular local Young Liberals (and here I stress *local* and *young*) really knew how to hate!

Baba had come through London during the first, February, campaign and greatly to the disapproval of the Party's agent in Norwood I had taken two days off from campaigning to be with him. Baba had advised me to go on doing my best but made it clear that in his view an election was an unimportant event in one's life, which should not be taken too seriously—wise words in retrospect but hard to bear in mind while the campaign was still on.

The second, October 1974 campaign in Norwood was notable as the first in which a candidate ran for the Gay Liberation Front. He and his supporters arrived for the Count in Lambeth Town Hall[9] wearing ankle-length robes of richly colored velvet, on which they had attached truncated extracts taken from some of our campaign publicity. It was all quite good-natured, as these events normally were, and although John Fraser's supporters were very worried by the GLF's intervention, fearing that it might have affected his not

---

9. In the U.K., voting is done with pencil and paper voting slips, which are sorted and counted. The 'Count' is attended by the candidates and party helpers, who can walk around the hall watching its progress. This system is still preferred.

very large majority, Ken Livingstone who was his agent at the time—later to become a member of Parliament himself and then a famous Mayor of London—had his Labour voters too well motivated for that to happen.

After that second 1974 election, faced with the possibility of four or five more years before another, I decided to look for a different line of work. I had found my two and a half years in active politics interesting and at the time imagined that I might find life worthwhile and stimulating as a member of Parliament. As a Party research officer one had had access to a particular row of seats in a discreet corner of the Chamber of the House and could attend any debate with a bearing on one's subjects of interest. With our passes, we could then go through the security checks in and out of the Parliament building and Committee Rooms with relative ease.

As an aspiring politician I had, though, to acknowledge in myself the serious flaw of not being at all sure of the answers to most of the country's problems—though I suppose time and experience would have helped. My main interest had anyway been more in world affairs. I used also to be irked by the insistence of my crafty, elderly boss in the Research Department that the documents we produced must include a significant element of party-political 'Labour-bashing'. Rather naively, perhaps, I thought that if our own policies were good, why not rely on them?

This boss was a great favorite with Margaret Thatcher and used to claim with obvious satisfaction that it was he who originally encouraged her to make her way in politics. To engage, as I believe Mrs. (later, Lady) Thatcher did, in the cut and thrust of political life to fight positively for remedies one can wholly believe in is surely the only honest reason for engaging in politics at all. However there were uncomfortably clear-cut differences between Mrs. Thatcher's approach, not least on Europe, and that of the defeated Heath administration with which I personally had been more able to identify.

In fact, soon after taking over as leader of the Conservative Party after its second 1974 electoral defeat, Mrs. Thatcher removed the Research Department from its separate premises and relocated it in the basement of Conservative Central Office in Smith Square where, no doubt, an eye could more easily be kept on it. Visiting a former colleague there some eighteen months later, I found that hardly any of the research staff I had known remained, such was the thoroughness of the new broom that had accompanied the change of leadership. Seemingly I had gone at the right time.

After cutting loose from the Research Department I took the opportunity of three more months with Baba and Savithri in Delhi, where Savithri now had a post as an assistant director in the Ministry of Labour. Baba was very busy at the time supervising the construction of his house in the Delhi suburb of Vasant Vihar. His design for the house was based on the Sanskrit letters for OM, so that the walls of the main building are curved; the design can be most clearly seen from the air. When first completed, Baba's house attracted considerable public attention. My part during the course of this work was to act for a while as Baba's driver, an enjoyable though sometimes alarming experience, particularly when the work took us into the narrow, crowded streets of Old Delhi where one was as likely to be avoiding a horse-drawn carriage, a bullock cart, pedestrians or a cow as another motor vehicle.

CHAPTER ELEVEN

The Next Phase Begins

Returning to England in mid-1975, I found a suddenly much tightened employment market. Eventually, an advertisement appeared in the *London Times* inviting applications for principal officer posts at an Equal Opportunities Commission, which was about to be set up in Manchester, in the northwest of England. A Sex Discrimination Bill had made its way through Parliament during the course of that year and the Commission would officially open its doors on December 29, 1975. In due course there were to be separate governmental commissions in Britain, one to deal with race relations and the other, the EOC, to deal with equality of opportunity and equal pay for women and men. Later still, the Commissions were amalgamated and given a different name so the stand-alone EOC no longer exists.

Not at all sure that I wanted to relocate from London to Manchester, and not yet even particularly aware of myself as a feminist, though I had absorbed almost at a gulp Germaine Greer's book, *The Female Eunuch*, then quite newly published, I thought these jobs looked promising, so applied. Baba, once again on his way through London, gave his blessing to the project by posting my application. In due course, I was interviewed by the newly appointed Chairman, her Deputy and a senior representative of the Home Office, the Commission's "parent" Department, and became one of the new Commission's Principals.

The British Sex Discrimination Act of 1975 was put together under the Right Hon. Roy Jenkins MP as Home Secretary. His Minister of State at the time who did much of the day-to-day work on the Bill as it went through Parliament was John Fraser, the same John Fraser who had been my political opponent in Norwood; while working to promote fairness in general, therefore, he had unknowingly done me personally a favor. I was really looking forward to a ministerial visit Mr. Fraser was to make to the Commission soon after it opened; at the last minute, however, he was reshuffled to another government department and the visit was called off.

Since all this was back in the early 1970s, it may be worth mentioning that the Act was devised as Britain's response to Article 119 of the 1957 Treaty of Rome, which was the treaty that had originally set up the European Economic Community. Article 119 required equal treatment in employment and equal pay for work of equal value for men and women. The British Act when it came also included equal treatment in education and in the provision to the public of facilities and services. Influenced by the American concept of less favorable treatment, established by the Supreme Court in 1971 in a race discrimination case[10], the British Act also defined unlawful indirect discrimination for the first time in British law. This refers to any practice or policy which on the surface appears to be even-handed but which, as previously explained, actually works disproportionately to the disadvantage of one affected group, and cannot be objectively justified.

---

10. Griggs v. Duke Power Company.

Being once again in at the beginning of a new enterprise was exhilarating. As one of the earliest Principal Officers in place my first task was to help those who were dealing with what we quickly termed the letter mountain, the correspondence that poured in to the Commission during the first weeks and months of its existence. This work was like undergoing a crash course on the astonishing range of discriminatory practices then existing. We had to work out the Act's likely application, if any, to all sorts of different complaints and queries.

Men, not surprisingly, leapt into the fray at once with a substantial spate of complaints about the discrepancy between the male and female State pension ages (then sixty-five and sixty respectively). However, those ages were laid down in previous legislation that the Sex Discrimination Act did not override and many years passed before the discrepancy was finally dealt with in such a way that no one really gained: women were granted the long-term prospect of waiting for their pensions up to the same age as men.

Field of Operations

Once all members of staff were in place, the three operational principals, of which I was one, were allotted their areas of responsibility. These would in each case cover England, Scotland and Wales. I had thought I might be given education but was not; since so much of my experience had been in the private sector, one could see why. Instead I was to deal with the application of the Act to how people were treated as users of services or facilities, including the Act's impact on employment advertising which in the early days of the Commission showed signs of being particularly resented as an intrusion. My brief soon developed to include some basically political concerns known internally as "other discrimination"; this involved pressing for amendment of the many discriminatory provisions in pre-existing laws which, as already mentioned, the new anti-discrimination law did not override.

Some Cases from Memory

Work at the EOC quickly became an absorbing interest. Only perusal of a dusty bookshelf-full of old annual reports would cover all the numerous cases fought and constructive changes achieved. A few early legal skirmishes in my own field of work stand out in memory.

Theresa Bennett

One memorable early case was that of Theresa Bennett, who was then eleven years old and very good at soccer. Her adult coach described Theresa as "a tigress in the field". Moreover, Theresa's school was small and Theresa was needed to make up their team, called Muskham United, in order to enter a junior league competition. At the time the teams were still all boys and the organizers would have none of it. Was Theresa not a *girl?* This was in 1976 and a film like "Bend It with Beckham" would have seemed to be light-years away and a Women's World Cup unimaginable.

The Commission decided to support Theresa's case. We reasoned that although there was an exception in the Act for sports where the average woman would be at a disadvantage to the average man by reason of physical strength or stamina, there was no evidence that the average eleven-year-old girl would necessarily be at such a disadvantage compared with a boy of the same age—in fact, sometimes the reverse might be true. The County Court judge agreed and found for Theresa. The EOC was suddenly unusually popular with the British press who, as I recall, were all in favor of our support for an eleven-year-old girl footballer.

Enter the football authorities, who seemed at the time to be passionately opposed to the idea of girls playing soccer, especially with boys. Perhaps they feared it might lead to women lining up for selection to play for Manchester United or Arsenal and objecting if they were not chosen. They mounted a serious rearguard action against the County Court decision and sadly Lord Denning, then Master of the Rolls and one of the most senior judges in England, decided when the first decision was appealed that he agreed with the football authorities. He decreed that the exception for sport meant that a female of any age must be compared with a male of any age; there could be no special consideration for a comparison of eleven-year-olds. Our good press in the matter disappeared overnight and now apparently we were wasting public money by supporting such a frivolous case.

Fortunately the cause of women's sport, including soccer, has moved on but a British government minister still felt it necessary to ask for a fairer share of media coverage for women following their remarkable performance at the London 2012 Olympics.

El Vino's

Another early case which invariably attracted press coverage was about the stuffy and patronizing treatment of women customers by a Fleet Street wine bar called El Vino's. At that time, London's Fleet Street was virtually synonymous with the British press, so the press could hardly fail to take an interest. In fact, when eventually the complainants, Tess Gill and Anna Coote, won their sex discrimination case against El Vino's this was the first and only case supported by the British EOC that I ever saw reported in the *Minneapolis Star Tribune*.

The problem was that the proprietors of El Vino's would not allow women customers to approach the bar and order drinks.

Women were told to go and find a seat at a table and wait to be served. All the news and gossip of the day would be discussed at the bar, so banning women reporters from participation was not only irritating but also to their professional disadvantage. Any policy by a service provider of treating customers differently according to gender was by then unlawful anyway unless there was a relevant exception in the Act.

As at a previous attempt, this case was lost in the lower court; however, this time the decision was appealed. There was near panic at the top of the Commission as the date of the appeal hearing approached; it was feared by some that the Court might find the issue *de minimis*—not important enough to merit attention. Much to my relief, a powerfully argued two-page memorandum from the then deputy chief executive, Dipak Nandy, carried the day and helped to keep the appeal on course. When the case came up before the judges, each of them began by declaring an interest: they were themselves customers of El Vino's—did either side in the dispute have any objection to that? Neither side did. The Court went on to uphold the appeal in favor of the complainants,

I heard a story, which I hope is true, that the mother of Harriet Harman MP used to tell her daughter, a lawyer and friend of the El Vino's complainants, that she could not understand what all the fuss was about. Then one day she happened to go into El Vino's and walked up to the bar to order a drink. The appeal had not yet been heard so of course she was subjected to the El Vino's treatment and told that, like it or not, as a woman she must go and sit down and wait to be served. To be treated in this way was not her style at all and she was incensed. She told her daughter that *now* she understood. This tale suggests that if people are to understand how galling some apparently insignificant acts of discrimination are, it may help to be on the receiving end of them.

James v. Eastleigh Borough Council

The approach taken by the British antidiscrimination legislation was logically evenhanded and this was an example of a case that was fought on behalf of men. Many British local authorities offered use of their amenities and services, such as bus and train travel, at discounted rates for older citizens. They did this at their own discretion and almost always linked the concessions to the different State pension ages of 60 for women and 65 for men. One can easily imagine how this might rankle—all the more so if a man had taken or had had to take early retirement.

Mr. James complained to the Commission that he had to pay the full rate for use of his local swimming pool while a woman of his age would pay only the concessionary rate. The difference might not be great but he objected on principle to the unfairness. The fact was that while the actual differing pension ages were not affected by the Act and there was an exception provided for employment policies linked to them, there was no such exception for the provision of services. Mr. James had raised an issue that deserved to be tested.

That simple case had to go all the way to the highest court in the land, then referred to as the House of Lords but now known as the Supreme Court. Possibly the other courts hesitated to find for Mr. James because of the widespread repercussions such an apparently small issue might have. The borough council threatened to increase the age for concessions for women or stop giving age concessions altogether; however local authorities are elected bodies and— as is becoming clearer by the day—the withdrawal of benefits once granted is not popular. Mr. James won his case by a majority decision in the Lords and from then on local authorities all over Britain had to devise ways of giving age concessions, if they chose to give them at all, on the same terms to men and women—a small but, surely, very justifiable success for the principle of equal treatment.

Formal Investigations

There was a view among some influential people at the Commission that it was important to make good use of a novel power the Commission had been given to conduct a legal process, described in detail in the Sex Discrimination Act and called a formal investigation. As a result, I often felt under pressure while at the Commission to make use of this power, which appropriately used could be a power for good but in my experience was generally not required for the sort of work I was doing.

If one could secure the legitimate objective of equal treatment without recourse to the formal investigation, or even the courts, that was obviously the best approach from everyone's point of view. When it was a question of the way people were treated as customers or users of services there was often no real, for which read financial, issue at stake, so persistent follow-up of casework, explanation of the law and discussion could frequently achieve the desired result. A discriminatory policy might only be surviving because of long-standing custom and practice; moreover, a change to equal treatment might often turn out to be not so much a hazard as good for business.

Only twice during all my years at the EOC was a formal investigation embarked on in relation to the provision of services. On the first occasion the investigation, dealing with retail credit, was called off almost at once because the large retail chain concerned offered full cooperation. On the second, when in my absence the Commission decided to pursue an investigation into a mortgage company's treatment of married women's income in mortgage assessments, its decision to investigate was challenged in the High Court, and that investigation too was called off. Then, everything was discussed, fair and workable guidelines were agreed and so far as I know there were no more similar complaints.

Insurance

Unequal treatment in insurance was another matter! Shared risk is the very essence of insurance but to include both sexes in the sharing was apparently unthinkable. Our handicap here was an exception included in the British Act by the Government Actuary of the day while the Bill was going through Parliament. This exception was made virtually bulletproof by use of the word reasonable, not once but twice in a single clause, so giving maximum leeway to the defense. After all, he was an actuary.

If equal treatment of men and women in insurance were to be introduced, there would have to be a legal requirement affecting all insurers at the same time—hence, the need for a test case. The Commission's best opportunity relating to insurance came when it backed Jennifer Pinder, a self-employed dentist, in a case against a large and well-known insurance company in 1983. Ms. Pinder had, as a woman, to pay considerably more for Permanent Health (also known as Disability Income) Insurance than a male colleague would pay. This type of insurance is used mainly by self-employed professionals and there were then very few women takers. There was no real need to make women pay so much more. In fact, a very senior actuary told me in confidence at about that time that if Mrs. Thatcher, then Prime Minister, had asked him what to do about equal treatment in insurance generally, he would have told her to go ahead with it since it was perfectly possible.

Jennifer Pinder's case failed not least because the expert witness who appeared for her and the Commission fell at the first fence. Asked, very reasonably, by a friendly sounding opposing Counsel whether the current practice of the insurers could not be seen as being reasonable, our witness replied thoughtfully that, yes, it was reasonable, but...And that was effectively the end of the case. The judge, in deciding for the insurers, took the view that they had necessarily to take a "broad brush" approach, which, in practice, meant that they could justify almost anything. When I told Baba what had happened, he told me not to worry, equal treatment would come eventually, though obviously not yet!

The European Court of Justice having in 2011 ruled at last for equal treatment of men and women in insurance, it will be interesting to see how in Britain the ruling is being implemented and to what extent the worst prognostications of some insurance practitioners are coming to pass. The most important long-term effect of this development should be on women's annuities—that is, their post-retirement incomes.

Clubs

Clubs can be very revealing in what they tell us about attitudes towards equality in society. The way various kinds of private members' clubs treated them was always a source of heartfelt complaints from women all over Britain. Some of the worst offenders were golf clubs and the traditional British Working Men's clubs. Genuinely private clubs whose members had to be proposed and seconded and approved by a committee were considered to be outside the scope of the sex discrimination law, so usually there was not much we could do to help.

If a genuinely private club or association was single sex there might not necessarily or always be a problem of discrimination. When clubs that were arguably private allowed women into membership but then denied them, as often happened, the same voting rights as men, there clearly was cause for complaint. The usual justification offered was that women benefited from a reduced membership fee—but neither men nor women had the option to pay more and get more or pay less and get less. Any progress would have to depend on the club members themselves, the women and any men whose support they could enlist and on changing perceptions and attitudes in society generally. With rare exceptions, the rate of change in the clubs while I was at the Commission was glacial, but perhaps it has speeded up since.

Other Discrimination

Those who originally devised social security schemes in Britain certainly did so with benevolent intent but, even after World War II, everything they did still reflected the assumption that the average British family would have a breadwinner husband with a dependent wife. Since by the 1970s more than half of married women were in paid employment, this meant that some rules had become plainly unjust. One by one those rules were amended—but usually only after reference to the European Court of Justice.

The laws on income tax reflected the same model. The married man's tax allowance was designed to help him meet the living expenses of two or more people. With so many two-income families this too had become an anomaly. Until well into the 1980s, a married woman's income had to be declared on her husband's income tax return, giving her no right to privacy in the matter at all. All this was for years the subject of public debate, in which the Commission naturally had its say, but in Britain independent taxation for married women was a long time coming. It was eventually tackled by a Conservative Chancellor, Nigel Lawson, later Lord Lawson, who started the process of reforming the system to make it work in a fairer, more gender-neutral way.

British nationality law too was long overdue for reform. In 1979 a newly elected Conservative government was revising nationality law for its own purposes and while this was happening we pressed for the patriarchal aspects of the old law to be removed as well. To ignore a mother's contribution to her child's nationality is patently absurd; until recently maternity was anyway more provable than paternity. From 1980, British nationality could be inherited through a parent or grandparent of either gender, instead of only through the male line. That was a particularly rewarding early success for the EOC.

Change of Direction

During my last few years at the Commission, I was given the chance to promote work and family issues which were being highlighted by the Commission's third chair, Joanna Foster. These included the need for good quality early childcare, maternity pay and maternity and paternity leave, and the right of mothers to return to work after childbirth—all very necessary and interesting initiatives and critical to women's chances of career development. Individual parents may or may not choose or need to work outside the home but readily available, reliable, affordable early childcare is essential if there is to be any real equality of opportunity. It must surely also be obvious that investing in a good start for all young preschool children needs to be very near the top of any country's list of national priorities.

Bowing Out Again

By the time I retired from the EOC in 1995 equality of opportunity in Britain had certainly made progress, though not everywhere and not necessarily at all income levels. Really equal opportunity, not to mention equal pay, will take longer. Worldwide, the terms and focus of the gender debate will no doubt continue to unfold, but a better and more humane balance of opportunity and freedom for all surely remains one of the most important and incompletely resolved issues of human justice facing the people of this planet.

CHAPTER TWELVE

The Other Side of the Picture

It will come as no surprise that throughout my years with the Equal Opportunities Commission I was constantly in touch with Baba by telephone and inwardly sustained by the prospect of the next occasion when I could spend some time with him. I would hoard my annual leave entitlement and take three, occasionally even four, weeks at a time so that I could be with Baba in India or, more usually, the United States. Baba would also regularly break his journeys between the United States and India and spend a few days with me in England. A few times we visited Scotland, which Baba once called the "Himalayas" of Britain and whose atmosphere he really liked.

Here I must emphasize again that this memoir only gives an account of a few of my own experiences with Baba. Even after I met Baba and became close to him, it will already be clear that for many years I was living and working in England, while almost all of his most important work in the world was done while he was in the United States or India; I heard about it but was not there to witness it. Moreover I cannot even attempt to describe or define Baba himself. I can only share my deep and undying love, fascination and wonder, my profound awareness of Baba's spiritual greatness and my conviction that his entire life was and is a gift and sacrifice for the ultimate good of everyone who came into contact with him personally, and of humanity as a whole.

Baba's invariable way of signing or autographing anything other than official documents was "All Love, BABA" and it was clear to me that a powerful assertion for justice was at the heart of everything he did. With that, Baba never wanted people around him to think of themselves as disciples, or himself to act holy. He was intensely practical and enjoyed the good things of life as much as anyone, while always liberally sharing whatever he had. Finally it should be remembered that from February 1962 to the end of his earthly life in March 2010, though he was very eloquent, travelled frequently and widely and achieved an extraordinary amount and range of work, Baba himself never uttered a word.

A Few of the Things That Happened

For many years most of the time I spent with Baba necessarily consisted of my allowance of annual leave, and as a result some of the incidents described below may seem on the face of it to be merely holidays. Though often quite strenuous, they were indeed holidays, but there was also in every case a deeper reason for what was happening. Baba did not waste time.

Once, while Baba was with me in England, he decided that we should drive to Paris to celebrate my birthday with Iranian friends who were living there at the time. Three of us went with Baba via the cross-Channel ferry (no Channel Tunnel then) and arrived in Paris at 3:00 a.m. when, to my relief as driver, there was practically no traffic on the streets. Baba's friends lived in a third-floor apartment near the Madeleine and at that hour we were able to park the car just below their windows. This was in 1982 and Baba was introduced by our hosts to a large and enterprising group of their compatriots who, like them, had taken refuge in Paris after the Ayatollah's revolution in Iran. Many were artists or musicians. There was talk and music late into the night and one could see that these exiles related instantly to Baba and were particularly moved and happy to be with him.

There was an amusing incident on our way back to England. We were three women traveling with Baba on that occasion, and as one after the other we walked into the bar on the ferry, the barman remarked in a very audible stage whisper to his colleague, "How *do* these Muslims do it?". Baba, when he was out and about, concealed his long hair with a neat woolen cap and was quite often taken for a Muslim, though in fact he could not be identified with any religion. Far from being offended, he was amused by this cheeky remark and promptly ordered drinks all round. Baba might choose to create a convivial atmosphere in an instant, whether with old friends or people meeting him for the first time.

Pilgrimage

Father had died in 1969, while I was still at Cobham Hall. Towards the end of 1986, when my mother was in a nursing home and very near death, Baba came to England with Renée to be with me. Previously, I had been with Baba and Renée in St. Paul when Renée had lost her mother prematurely to cancer. Soon after my mother's funeral, Renée returned to the Twin Cities and Baba took me with him to India on a pilgrimage to the main places connected with each of the spiritual Masters in his line. This time Baba made a point of going via Moscow. This was in January 1987, and the Soviet Union was still intact. Traveling by Aeroflot, we found we could arrange an organized transit weekend in Moscow, for which we needed special visas. Obtaining these proved to be a saga in itself but we secured them in the end and soon were on our way.

On arrival in Moscow our passports were impounded, as was the practice, to be retrieved by us only when we returned to the airport to leave. We were taken by bus to a hotel and given accommodation high above the city. As we emerged onto the twenty-seventh floor, there sat the customary elderly woman keeping watch on all who came and went. Before we left England, I had shown Baba the fox-fur hat I was taking to wear in Moscow, and he had thought it a great joke. No sooner had he experienced the Moscow winter, however, (in which everyone was wearing a fur hat of some kind) than he decided that fur hats were not such a bad idea.

The Intourist guide who was helping us, a delightful woman who spoke excellent English and moved with the grace of a ballerina, told us how to find the tourist shop where we could buy a hat for Baba and there we went at once. I had thought the assistants in a tourist shop would be interested and keen to sell; not a bit of it. They seemed bored and apathetic, and we had difficulty in persuading anyone even to show us what they had to offer. In the end, we managed to buy a handsome brown Astrakhan hat for Baba, which he wore outside from then on until we reached India. He was still wearing that hat at the airport in Delhi and, for a moment, even Savithri had difficulty recognizing him.

At this time, there was much talk of *glasnost* and *perestroika*, but nothing much had changed yet. There seemed to be very little to buy in the shops and the hotel food was not at all appetizing. In the evening, Baba asked me to wrap up warmly and go out to buy some fruit. Having come to Moscow, for his own reasons he may have needed some time alone, though it would not be surprising if after seeing the hotel fare he had also wanted some fruit. So I set off, fur hatted and booted and in my warm coat, to find a fruit shop or supermarket. At the hotel I was told to take a certain bus for a few stops until I saw a wide, open square where there would be a super-market. Boarding the bus, I realized I had no idea how to pay any fare; however, no one was talking and no one paid any attention to me so I never paid anything.

Coming to what I thought must be the square in question, I got off the bus and started tramping through foot-deep snow towards some lights on the far side. Sure enough, this turned out to be a small food market. Inside there were quite a few customers looking at the almost barren shelves and again, it was very noticeable that no one was saying a word. The only flurry of activity was round a heap of fresh lemons that people were seizing and putting into brown paper bags. Searching around for more fruit, all I could find was some apples that looked like elderly Golden Delicious; I put some in a bag and went to join the silent line for checkout. Without a word the woman at the checkout weighed the apples, took my money, handed me some change and the deed was done.

Now the problem was to find my way back to the hotel. I took a bus that I guessed was going back the way I had come, but after about a block it turned to the right and swept down towards the river. I got off as soon as I could and trudged back about a quarter of a mile through the snow to the main road, where I risked taking another bus, which luckily kept going in the right direction. Before long, I spotted our hotel, got off the bus at the next stop and stag-gered across to the hotel entrance, arriving upstairs at last with my precious bag of apples for Baba. He looked at them, looked at me, and signed, "Is that *all?*" I had to laugh! I felt I had accomplished a bold and strenuous feat out there on my own in the freezing Moscow night, much complicated by my inability to read any signs or speak a word of Russian.

Our kind Intourist guide arranged for us to go to see Red Square, and from the outside, St. Basil's Cathedral. We could of course also glimpse the onion towers behind the great Kremlin walls and observe the straggling line of people, huddled and stamping in the cold, waiting to visit Lenin's tomb. She also arranged for us to attend a performance at the Bolshoi Theatre on the Sunday evening. I remember the setting well, but for some reason can remember almost nothing of the performance except that it was not a ballet. Baba invited our guide to join us for a drink at any time or place convenient to her, but she told us sadly that if she did such a thing she would lose her job.

On that guide's recommendation too, we went on the Sunday morning to visit, just outside the city, a complex of buildings, including churches, which had belonged to the Tsar. When we arrived, we found the main church building open and packed with people; there was incense and deep-voiced chanting. In one aisle of the church, there was the body of an old woman displayed in an open coffin on a kind of catafalque; by the time we left, the old woman's body had been removed. There were other buildings round about, and we went across to another church where we found the great wooden doors heavily chained and padlocked. Baba asked me to take a photograph of him standing with his back to those locked doors. We were using a Polaroid camera and the cold was so intense that the fluid on the photograph froze as it emerged from the camera so that what might have been a historic picture was partly spoiled.

Having come by taxi, I was keen to try the underground on our way back into town and Baba kindly indulged me. This was fine except for our well-known inability to read the signs and the fact that, at that time, no one we asked spoke a word of anything but Russian. We had no way of knowing which might be the station nearest to our hotel, so after a few stops, we got off the train and took a taxi for the rest of the way. At least, I had experienced the famous Moscow Underground.

On our return to the airport the next evening we had to wait a very long time indeed to retrieve our passports because those who were giving them out had to go through the entire pile every time to find the relevant passport for each passenger. After a further long wait for our flight we were on the plane to Delhi at last, our brief but eventful visit to Moscow behind us. Baba told me that he had had a particular wish to visit Russia at least once.

On to India

On the plane between Moscow and Delhi, a young woman from Sweden was in the seat next to Baba; she told us her name was Eva. She was traveling alone and seemed to be rather sad so Baba befriended her and invited her to stay with us, which she did. She was with Baba, Savithri and me in Savithri's Curzon Road apartment in Delhi, accompanied the three of us on our pilgrimage and all the way to Prasanth, where she stayed for two or three weeks before leaving to see more of Kerala to the south. Eva created quite a stir one day in Prasanth, having gone off to a lonely spot on the estate for some sunbathing in the nude. Workers came running in consternation to tell Baba they had seen the dead body of a woman near some trees! Not a lot of sunbathing, nude or otherwise, is done in the Kerala countryside.

We had only stayed in Delhi long enough to secure, as we thought, four sleeper tickets for the train journey south to Manmad, the nearest station to Shirdi where we would visit Sai Baba's tomb. This train journey turned out to be quite an unusual experience. When the train stopped at a place called Jhansi, an elderly gentleman with his wife and another woman came on board and claimed that we were sitting in their seats. They called the ticket collector and showed their tickets. We showed our tickets, which they claimed could not be valid. We were determined not to be decanted onto the platform at Jhansi late at night and held our ground.

The train was packed and everyone around started to join in the argument so that a considerable commotion built up. A posse of Jhansi police even appeared, rather ominously, on the platform outside. When the fun had started, Eva had sensibly climbed onto an upper bunk and lay there, peacefully observing all that was going on. The train was held up because of all this for about an hour and the other passengers were becoming very upset about the delay. Eventually, the matter was settled, though we lost our sleeper accommodation for most of the night and had to manage with seats that were somehow found for us. At last the train pulled out of the station, mercifully with Baba, Savithri, Eva and me still on board. With the trains so fully booked, we might have been stranded in Jhansi for days. As we left the train in Manmad Baba, with the merest hint of a twinkle in his eye, solemnly advised the elderly gentleman who had ousted us to take special care of his health for one year.

Shirdi–Our Pilgrimage Proceeds

At Manmad we took a taxi to Shirdi and checked in at a hotel. At 4:00 a.m. next day we walked through the town to attend the morning *arti* (prayer and praise) at Sai Baba's tomb. On the way, Baba bought a large basket full of fresh, red rose petals for Sai Baba. When we arrived, the temple was already filling up and more people were arriving all the time. Baba joined the crowd of men on the left, and we three women sat down with all the other women on the right. Attendants were walking up and down receiving offerings of flowers, rose water, whatever people had brought to offer. The music and singing started, and then began a ritual bathing of Sai Baba's more than life-sized marble statue—I saw that this was why people had brought rose water. At the end, first all the men and then all the women moved slowly forward to bow at the tomb, a solemn moment in an atmosphere of great devotion. People from all over India had come for this, and not only from India, for other foreigners were to be seen here and there among the crowd.

Next, we went to visit Upasini Baba's ashram in Sakori, about three miles away. Godavari Mataji and the *kanyas* (the women who were living a dedicated life at the ashram) were overjoyed to see Baba and Savithri and welcomed us all very kindly. We were given lunch and a large room to rest in. We were shown all around the ashram and visited the ashram temple and Upasini Baba's living area, where we saw the cage in which he once for a period confined himself and where I was particularly touched to see his sandals, lovingly preserved. Before we left we attended the evening *arti,* or worship, in the temple, at which Godavari Mataji presided.

Also present at the ashram was one of the *kanyas* called Geeta. We could tell that Geeta, now well on in years, was especially happy to see Baba again. When Baba, known at the time as Krishnaji, had been sent by Meher Baba in 1952 to pave the way for him to re-visit Sakori, Baba had been instrumental in curing Geeta from both terminal cancer and tuberculosis.

On his arrival in Sakori on that occasion Baba had found a very somber atmosphere, since all at the *ashram* knew that Geeta was mortally ill. Asking to be taken to see the patient, he had approached her bedside, picked up the bowl of blood and sputum beside her, drunk its entire contents, reassured Geeta that God would help her and all would be well, and left the room. Geeta had then begun to recover and here she was, welcoming Baba to Sakori in 1987. Needless to say, when Meher Baba had subsequently visited Sakori for the first time as a Baba, he was received by all there with love and profound reverence.

After our brief stay in Sakori, we drove on to Meherabad to visit Meher Baba's tomb. Here on that particular day there seemed to be few people about. We were received by a young man of western appearance, who instructed us to bow down at the tomb and gave each of us a toffee. Remembering the heaps of flowers and the crowds of worshippers we had seen at Shirdi and the warmth of our welcome at Sakori, it was a little sad to see just a few faded flowers in a vase near the tomb and so few people about; however, we had come to bow at Meher Baba's tomb and that we happily did.

Next there was another quite long drive to Poona, now Pune, where we spent the night with Savithri's brother and his family. On the following day, we visited the tomb of Hazrat Babajan, the "ancient woman" Perfect Master, or *sadguru,* who had first awakened Meher Baba to his spiritual status and destiny. Babajan's tomb was fenced off near a great, old tree in what is now quite a busy part of town, under which tree for many years she would remain seated day and night and in all weathers. Babajan was known to have had a particular love of tuberoses and people still bring them to her tomb, which was then being looked after by an elderly attendant who greeted Baba and all of us warmly. For several hours after our visit to Babajan's tomb the scent of tuberoses stayed with us.

Belgaum and Shanti Bastwad

Our last stop before Bangalore where our pilgrimage would end was in Belgaum, a town near the border between the States of Maharashtra and Karnataka. Near Belgaum was a village called Shanti Bastwad, where as a young man of twenty-four, some thirty years previously, Baba had spent several months living as a beggar. In Belgaum, we stayed with the family of a man named Bharatbhai, who all those years ago had seen Baba sitting under a tree by the side of the road near Shanti Bastwad, had stopped his car and invited Baba to his home, from then on insisting that Baba must stay in his home every weekend. By this time Bharatbhai had died but his widow and other members of the family were there. It was clear that all of them were happy and excited by Baba's arrival, whether they had only heard about him or were old enough to remember him.

Our visit to Shanti Bastwad next day was one of the most memorable occasions I have ever witnessed. Baba had first come there in 1954, with nothing but the cotton robe he was wearing. By day he had sat under the tree and at night he had gone to a disused mosque. By the time he left after some three months, he had become so beloved that every man in the village had taken it in turns to fast for a day to persuade him to return and stay with them permanently. After they had kept this up for six months, Baba had had to go back to the village and explain that he had much work to do in the world and that it was not God's will that he should remain in Shanti Bastwad; they must not continue to fast.

This time when he came everyone concerned with his previous visit was half a lifetime older, but clearly no one had forgotten. So much in the life of the village was the same, so much had changed. As soon as recognition dawned, the excitement was intense. We could see people running from house to house to pass on the news. Old, faded photographs of their younger selves standing with Baba as they remembered him were brought out in each house—simple, village homes, some with dirt floors and sacks of grain stacked inside, where the photographs were fetched from the rafters; some more elaborate homes now with wooden floors and verandas. Each had its treasured memento to show Baba.

One who particularly begged Baba to come to his house was the village blacksmith. When Baba accepted his invitation, the blacksmith ran ahead to make his preparations. As Baba approached the door of his home, the blacksmith would not allow Baba to enter the house before he had asked him to stand on a small, wooden platform so that he could reverently wash and dry Baba's feet with his own hands, and place a hibiscus flower between the first and second toe of each foot. Only then did he bow low and show Baba into his house. It was a deeply touching experience to see how this humble blacksmith in a quiet village in the heart of India received Baba after an absence of more than thirty years.

After we left Belgaum, we drove on to Bangalore and spent a day there with Baba's oldest and closest friends, Raju and Muthu Rajaram, and their family before taking the overnight train from Bangalore to Mangalore. From there, a car took us the sixty miles to Prasanth for some quiet, peaceful days with Baba's parents.

CHAPTER THIRTEEN

In the United States with Baba

My many visits to be with Baba were, as we know, the highlights of my year and in Minnesota, as in India, whether we stayed at home or traveled, the visits were always memorable. During the days of the Ruby Cup business, much of the time would be spent either in the Twin Cities, where the main business was based, or with Isabelle Thorson and her family in the country town of Blooming Prairie, from where it was an easy drive to Baba's Shop in Rochester, Minnesota.

At one time Baba acquired near the Twin Cities, in a town called Eden Prairie, Everblooms, a business with thirty-six thousand rose bushes under glass; this was a demanding enterprise requiring twenty-four-hour attention, especially in the freezing Minnesota winters. Beautiful, long-stemmed roses were grown and marketed and any left unsold were gathered up from the cold rooms and distributed by Baba personally to old people in care homes round about. Their appreciation was very evident and they must have sorely missed those visits when eventually that business was sold and, later, demolished to make way for new development.

The man who had originally built up the rose garden had had the excellent idea of incorporating a small swimming pool as an extension of the heated glasshouses. In 1979, when I had gone to spend Christmas and the New Year with Baba, we celebrated around that swimming pool with a large party of Baba's workers, friends and their children, surrounded by luxuriant, tropical plants, with the temperature outside at minus nineteen degrees Fahrenheit.

Round the States by Amtrak

One January, Baba asked me to bring with me from England two special tickets being marketed to foreign tourists visiting the States. These tickets were offered at a very good price and allowed one to travel by Amtrak, the United States passenger rail service, anywhere one liked, stopping wherever one liked, provided the journey was completed within a month. Bookings for each stage were necessary because the seats on the trains were allocated in advance. We managed to obtain a similar pass for Renée on the ground that she was needed to interpret for Baba, and the three of us set off from Minneapolis on a circular trip round the States.

Our journey took us through Chicago to Ann Arbor, Michigan, then to Buffalo, New York, to Boston and Lexington, Massachusetts, then on via the spectacularly decorated station at Washington DC, to Charlottesville, Virginia (from where we were able to visit Monticello, the lovingly preserved home of Thomas Jefferson), from Charlottesville to New Orleans, then west past the Texas oil wells, dipping and raising their birdlike bills, and on through Arizona to Los Angeles where we spent four or five days. After that, we were back on the train with the Pacific coastline to our left, towards our last stop in San Francisco to be with friends in Oakland, California—whose house, it was discovered while we were there, was right beside one belonging to Meher Baba. After that we headed back to Minneapolis, pausing only to change trains in Portland, Oregon.

At each place where we stopped—apart from New Orleans where we stayed at a hotel, went out and about, visited the French Quarter and generally enjoyed the atmosphere, music and food—we were received at the stations by and stayed with friends of Baba. Every one of those stops was full of interest, each in its own way. Mostly we did not do or see spectacular things (though we did see spectacular things, like the Niagara Falls, the Golden Gate Bridge at San Francisco and Thomas Jefferson's Monticello) so much as spend time with our hosts and their families, all of whom wanted to make as much as they could of their opportunity to be with Baba. Between stops we spent days and nights on the trains, which had comfortable reclining seats, very good dining cars and observation lounges, and bunks which could be hired at extra cost if required. Two or three times we took a bunk for Baba who endured pain in his knees, but Renée and I were fine with the comfortable seats.

Baba certainly had his own reasons for undertaking this journey and Renée and I just had the benefit of accompanying him. On the long, last lap through the Rocky Mountains and the northern plains back to Minneapolis, I was watching anxiously a massive storm that seemed to be pursuing us. My return flight to Manchester was booked for the day after we were due to reach Minneapolis, and I was expected back at the office the day after that. Luckily, the storm held off until we were safely home, and since probably no airport in the United States is better at managing severe weather conditions than Minneapolis/St. Paul, I was back in Manchester on time.

Barbados

On another of my visits to the States, when my right wrist was in a plaster cast following a fall while walking on the hills of the Peak District in Cheshire, Baba decided to use some complimentary air tickets he had to visit Barbados. In the end, there were seven of us in the party. I had to leave Barbados after the first week, but not before Baba arranged for a very kind doctor from Kerala named Meerabai, sister-in-law of the Chief Justice of Chennai and a good friend ever since, to have the plaster removed from my wrist. This was done with the help of an enormous pair of shears and involved some quite alarming struggle, but once my wrist was intact and liberated I could strengthen it with some sea bathing before heading back to England, this time through Miami.

Everybody in the party loved Barbados. Baba found an apartment near the sea, which comfortably accommodated all of us. We bought wonderfully fresh fish, fruit, and vegetables from the markets and usually did our own cooking. As usual, Baba took charge of most of it. Baba often prepared delicious meals of fish or fowl for others but was vegetarian himself. With the abundance of coconuts and other tropical fruits everywhere around, Baba in particular felt very much at home; it was all so reminiscent of Kerala. We traveled around the island by bus and saw the main towns and sights, we enjoyed the sea and the sun, and Baba met many people and made many friends. On my last evening we had dinner at a seafood restaurant on a terrace overlooking the sea, as the sun went down in a blaze of color. I have no doubt that, as ever, Baba had his own reasons for this visit to Barbados, possibly to do with the ongoing US-led invasion just about then of Grenada. He alone knew his reasons, which might become evident only later, even many years later—but the trip to Barbados resulted for the rest of us in a fine holiday.

Denver, Tucson, and Las Vegas, New Mexico

On yet another occasion, when this time Savithri was with us in the States, Baba went by car with Savithri, Renée and me to Tucson, Arizona, to visit John Donohue, a good friend who had been the founder of the famous Children's Theatre in Minneapolis. John, an extremely talented producer, was then working at a theatre in Tucson. On our first evening there we saw his production of a stage version of Dickens's *Great Expectations*; the whole performance was remarkable and I was also much impressed by the actors' command of the Kentish accent in English.

On our way to Tucson we stopped at Denver, Colorado, to meet the owners, Mr. and Mrs. Hirschfeld, of the monumental, thirteen-foot-by-seven-foot portrait of Baba by the well-known American photorealist artist, Audrey Flack. Baba had been invited to attend as guest of honor a large function in their mansion. Before attending the function we went to hear Audrey addressing students at the nearby University of Boulder, Colorado. Audrey had not known that Baba would come to hear her and when he walked in at the back of the hall she exclaimed in delighted surprise and introduced him to her audience as the subject of her painting, *Baba*, a slide of which featured in the course of her talk. (For the portrait, see pages 194-5.)

Baba's portrait had been bought by Mr. Hirschfeld on the first day on which it had been exhibited in New York. This was the first time that Savithri and I had seen the actual painting, though we had long been familiar with photographs of it. The Hirschfelds' spacious home was faithfully modeled on the set of Shangri-La in the 1930s film of James Hilton's novel *Lost Horizon*. The portrait had been hung against the white wall of a magnificent, broad, curved stairwell where it could be seen in very good light by anyone entering the house. It was destined eventually for public display and, indeed, was reported in early 2012 to have been donated by Barry and Arlene Hirschfeld to the Butler Institute of American Art, in Youngstown, Ohio.

On driving through New Mexico on our way home we were caught in a blizzard. There were numerous cars already stranded in ditches on either side of the road as we crawled along in very poor visibility. After several minutes of this, we saw a motel near the road and Baba decided we should stop there for the night. This was no five-star establishment, but it was warm and safe. Its location turned out to be a small town called Las Vegas—a very modest Las Vegas compared with its namesake in Nevada.

The motel was being run by a young couple from India and next morning, when Baba and Renée went to pay for our rooms, they found the manager's wife touchingly happy to meet Baba. It turned out that she was a devotee of Sai Baba of Shirdi and had been praying to Sai Baba for help, because her husband was not treating her well and had become violent; she was thousands of miles from her home and family, extremely unhappy and did not know what to do. She begged Baba to help her.

Baba spoke to the husband and told him that if he laid his hand in anger on his wife again, he, Baba, would see that he lived to regret it. A man from India would understand such a warning from Baba— he touched Baba's feet and promised that there would be no more such incidents. So an unhappy young woman, isolated in a lonely motel near a small town in New Mexico, USA, prays fervently to Sai Baba for help, and it so happens that during a blizzard Mouni Baba decides to stop at that motel. Each one can make of that what he or she will.

CHAPTER FOURTEEN

Love and Justice

As must already be evident, Renée Reed played a vital role in all of Baba's work in the United States. She accompanied him and interpreted for him continuously and at all hours, combining this with her full-time employment as a librarian, and was particularly engaged in his work for peace and justice for African Americans.

One high point of this work was a "Peace Summit" in St. Paul in July 1993, at which Baba brought together about a thousand multiethnic and multifaith gang leaders, men and women, from cities all across the United States—the majority of them African American, but including also Latinos and Caucasians. In response to their expressed concerns, Baba asked the police not to meddle and to leave the management of the meeting to him. The three-and-a-half-day event passed off without a single act of aggression or disruption of any kind, while generating instead a very powerful spirit of love, goodwill and reconciliation. This event grew out of Baba's work over several years with the internationally famous football player, Jim

Brown, to help gang leaders and members from South Central Los Angeles. Renée had been assured by Baba that before the end of her life an African American would be elected as President of the United States of America, something which she has said seemed to her at the time to be way beyond the realm of possibilities.

While numerous people, men and women, from many different backgrounds and nationalities were befriended by Baba and received his loving help, latterly only a handful of women without personal family responsibilities actually lived with him: one Indian (Savithri), one African American, one White American, one East European, and one Englishwoman. Each of them came to him at a critical point in her life, was accepted by him as family and received from then on his unfailing help and support.

As has already been stated, a powerful assertion for justice lay at the heart of almost everything Baba did and it is, therefore, not surprising that this had repercussions at a personal level for some of those who were close to him. Baba's support of my working for the Equal Opportunities Commission in England was consistent with this. For many years, also, an important preoccupation during my visits to be with Baba in Minnesota would be some ongoing lawsuit in which, much against her personal inclination, Renée found herself embroiled. In each case with Baba's constant help and encouragement she prevailed.

The first was no exception. This was a rape case brought in the civil court by Renée against a St. Paul medical doctor. In this instance the doctor countersued, alleging defamation by Baba because of his support for Renée.

When the case was due to come up in court, I made sure I was in Minneapolis. There was some delay, as is not unusual, and since the end of my leave was approaching, Renée's attorney, Bruce Douglas, subpoenaed me to stay and give evidence which he thought would be helpful. In a case depending largely on the credibility of the opposing parties, any relevant outside evidence is welcome.

Before the hearing Bruce, who had great love for Baba, pointed out that since he was representing Renée he could not also act for Baba; Baba must enlist the help of his own attorney. This Baba declined to do, saying he would represent himself. When, however, the hearing started and the doctor's attorney argued that if Baba would not speak he should not be allowed to give evidence since no one else in court could understand his sign language, Bruce was on his feet in an instant. He insisted that it was absurd to suggest that a man who had kept silence for more than twenty years should be required to speak, while it was a basic tenet of American jurisprudence that a defendant must be allowed to defend himself. All parties retired to the Judge's Chambers where it was decided that Baba would give his evidence in writing, to be read out to the court. Both sides in this dispute had agreed to dispense with a jury and rely on the judge sitting alone.

The entire proceedings in court—Renée's case against the doctor and the doctor's against Baba—lasted eight days. There were many unforgettable scenes and tense moments as, for example, when the doctor's attorney wanted Baba to answer yes or no to some characteristically complicated questions and Baba replied that if he had a question to ask in one word, he would answer in one word. The judge asked the attorney to be more reasonable but there was a point when he summoned a bailiff to the courtroom in case he should be needed. At the end of the session, Baba gave that officer a charming smile and a hug. The officer, a tough-looking individual, cannot often have been hugged in the course of his duties and may have been unsure what to make of it, though he looked pleased.

In questioning Baba, the doctor's attorney at one point asked him if he loved Renée. Baba wrote and his answer was read out, "Yes."

"Do you love Sam?" (Sam was Renéés father.)

"Yes."

"Do you love Bruce?"

"Yes."

"Do you love the doctor?"

"Yes."

"Do you love me?"

"Yes"—pause for writing and then—"I love you as the tiger loves the deer!"

Everyone in court laughed.

After prolonged and often distressingly ugly questioning of Renée by the defense attorney, that attorney called several people to give evidence on behalf of the doctor. This prolonged the proceedings but since it became clear that they had no firsthand witness to offer but only opinions, nothing very useful came of it.

In the end, the judge reserved his decision. When it came, he had dismissed the case against Baba and found for Renée, awarding her a relatively modest but far from derisory sum in compensation. What mattered was that Renée had been believed; moreover, doctors in the United States are a powerful group and to have succeeded in such an action against a doctor was a rare achievement.

While this was going on, back at the EOC in Manchester, England, the chief executive, herself a lawyer, was consulting the Civil Service rule book. She found that an officer must be given leave of absence to respond to a subpoena in a criminal case but might be required to do so with unpaid leave in a civil case. Accordingly, on my return to the office she docked me of two weeks' pay, though she did allow the sum to be deducted in monthly installments. It had been well worth it.

Case No. 2: The Library

Renée's next fight was with her employers at the Minneapolis Public Library. For thirteen years she, with very good qualifications and experience and despite consistently favorable performance reviews from her supervisors, was kept at entry level while white people, including some Renée herself had trained, were promoted over her. Renée's mother had been for many years a respected senior librarian at the St. Paul Public Library, where the atmosphere and attitudes were very different. At the Minneapolis Library, no black librarian had been appointed to a senior position in a hundred years.

The City of Minneapolis Human Rights Department prepared a long and detailed report that concluded that on three out of four counts there was probable cause for a charge of discrimination by the library. The director of the library nevertheless refused to negotiate and would neither discuss nor distribute to the members of her publicly elected Library Board a summary of the report, copies of which were made available to her by a city counselor. Over several months many people, myself included, tried to persuade those responsible at the library to take the matter seriously. It seemed that unless Renée was to remain at entry level for the rest of her time at the library and, also importantly for Renée, unless the prospects there for any employees of color were to remain unchanged, a formal complaint of racial discrimination was unavoidable.

For this, Renée clearly needed the help of a powerful attorney. Bruce was no longer available and Baba was able to enlist the support of another outstanding Minnesota civil rights attorney, Steve

Cooper. This at last caused the library authorities to take notice. A series of motions brought by the library were in all cases found in Renée's favor and, after many delays and callous, last-minute postponements, finally all parties met to negotiate and a settlement was reached. Renée was given a thirteen-step promotion and a considerable lump-sum payment in compensation for the unfair treatment which it was now acknowledged that she had suffered. Her own prospects had been transformed but she later observed with sadness that the general situation for minority employees at the Minneapolis Public Library hardly changed in the years following her case, which ended in 1993.

Case No. 3: A Border Dispute

After cases 1 and 2, Renée must have felt sure that her brushes with litigation were at an end, but it was not to be so. In 1995, Baba and Renée relocated from a rented apartment in St. Paul to a new home in New Brighton, a northern suburb of St. Paul. They bought the house from friends, making the decision to buy in about five minutes one Sunday morning. Within a day, papers were signed and the deal was settled.

In that particular enclave in New Brighton, Baba and Renée were the first people of color to purchase a property. The dispute that arose was never explicitly racially motivated but I have never doubted that that was what it was. Sometimes it may be the children who give the game away. They hear their parents and other adults talking and proceed to act out accordingly.

The house is near a corner of the road where the school bus stopped to pick up several children who lived nearby. No sooner had Renée and Maria, a white Minnesotan also living with Baba, moved into the house—Baba being at the time in India—than children started to throw their empty pop cans and other trash onto our lawns and drive, only. The attitude was obvious. After several days, Maria was ready for them. She boarded the bus and demanded that whichever child had thrown the last can onto our lawn get down from the bus and remove it. The driver of the bus backed Maria and eventually a shame-faced boy stood up and did as Maria demanded. After this, the head of the school was informed of the problem and arranged a different pickup point for the bus and that nuisance ended.

Everything then seemed to settle down, but it did not last. Suddenly, one day, the neighbors on one side came through the remains of a fence, which the previous owners of our house had for twenty-five years treated as the border between the properties, and started hacking at some bushes on our side. In answer to objections, they claimed that they were on their own land. If that were the case, it would not have been possible to walk on that side from the front of Baba's house to the back. Bylaws also required a minimum space between a residential building and the border of a property.

These neighbors had several times visited and taken coffee or a drink with Baba. Baba invited them to come again and discuss the situation, saying that if there had been a mistake, he and Renée would be happy to negotiate a fair settlement. A local counselor intervened and attempted to mediate, as did the mayor of New Brighton. For whatever reason, our neighbors suddenly refused to communicate except through a third party and stated in writing that they were not prepared to part with "an inch" of their land. Since the land they were claiming was important to us while because of where it was in relation to their house it was of no practical importance to them, a dispute was again inevitable.

At the outset we tried to manage without an attorney, spending hours preparing and responding to interrogatories ourselves. At some point, we became aware of a law of "adverse possession" according to which, if someone looked after land as his own for fifteen years or more without objection from the original owner, as had happened in this case, the occupier could claim it as his own. It seemed our position was stronger in law than we had known.

Not long after the other side engaged the services of a large law firm, Baba met and befriended yet another outstanding attorney, Clinton McLagan, who with a colleague had written the standard work on real estate law in general use by the legal profession in Minnesota. He agreed to act for Baba and Renée if and when necessary.

At a preliminary hearing that, it seemed to me, the neighbors approached with a display of great confidence, the judge, after listening carefully, said she thought the matter eminently suitable to be dealt with by means of arbitration. An arbitrator was, therefore, appointed and a day was set.

On the appointed day, the arbitrator shuttled backwards and forwards with admirable patience between the parties in separate rooms for several hours. He must finally have succeeded in convincing the other side of the relevance to this dispute of the law on adverse possession, for in the end it was agreed that the boundary between the properties would remain where it had effectively been for many years and also that the neighbors would replace the broken-down old fence with a new one in its original position. Each party was to pay its own costs. Thus, Baba and Renée, who had made it plain from the outset that, whatever the situation in law, they were willing to make any reasonable payment to avoid a dispute, ended up with costs approximating what they would anyway have been ready to pay. What the other side's costs were we do not know; we only know that they were unnecessary.

We were aware of a certain amount of gossip in the immediate locality while this dispute was going on, some though not all of it unfriendly, but we ignored it. Baba carried on beautifying the property with new lawns and landscaping to his own design, while continuing to produce his annual display of luxuriant flowers and other plants. Later, he for his own reasons added a copper roof to the house and some copper siding. Later still he transformed the entrance to the house with a totally redesigned porch, cladding its outer walls in fine Rainbow granite from central Minnesota. Instead of worrying about their new neighbors, all who lived nearby could have been proud and happy to welcome them.

Maria's Story

Maria had first come to hear about Baba through her husband, Roger, a successful agent for a large Midwestern insurance company. The couple lived on a sixty-acre farm in beautiful countryside near Monticello, Minnesota, about thirty miles northwest of the Twin Cities. This was where Maria had been raised from early childhood by foster parents who later adopted her, and it was from them that she and Roger had eventually bought the farm. Roger had been greatly taken with Baba and encouraged Maria to go to see him.

At the time, Maria was totally exhausted. She and Roger had been married for seventeen years and they had had two daughters, the elder of whom was very severely disabled and needed constant care. For years, Maria had singlehandedly looked after this daughter, Roger and her younger daughter, while contriving also to look after the farm and even to do night work in order to supplement their income. She came to visit Baba and Renée and quickly became a regular visitor to their home.

Roger had been very resistant to the idea of putting their daughter into care but Baba persuaded him that Maria had done at least as much for her as any mother could be expected to do, and that the time had come to relieve Maria of the heavy and lonely burden she had been carrying. This was in the early 1990s, when the elder girl was about twelve years old; from then on she was cared for by the State of Minnesota.

For many reasons, the marriage had been under strain. Baba, being close to both parties, tried for months to keep it together. One day Maria went to see Roger in his office to make one further attempt at reconciliation. When she arrived she was handed at the door a set of divorce papers. She was effectively homeless. There was a long waiting list at the women's refuges and she had nowhere to go and no source of income so she came back to Baba, and Baba and Renée agreed to share their home with Maria and her younger daughter while the divorce went through. What was expected to be a relatively short process lasting a few months turned into a marathon lasting eight and a half years. Maria's younger daughter went after two or three months to live with her father and Maria stayed with Baba and Renée and remained with them for many years as a member of the family.

The story of that divorce with all its twists and complications could almost fill a book. Roger's liking for Baba did not survive Baba's help and support of Maria. After many months, the divorce settlement ordered by the court gave Roger the couple's biggest asset, his business. Maria, although by then she was not the custodial parent, was awarded the house and farm, which she was planning to run for profit after a necessary preliminary period of development, in order to become financially independent. With the farm came, according to the court, the farm equipment and machinery; mysteriously all these essential items disappeared before Maria could take possession of them and there appeared to be no authority to which she could turn for help in retrieving them. Naturally, this ruined her chances of developing the farm.

The farm had also come with a sizeable outstanding mortgage, with monthly payments which would have wiped out the maintenance Maria was awarded for a limited time until, supposedly, she could become self-sufficient. Arrears of that maintenance built up and Maria had to apply to the court once more in order to secure their payment. An attorney then presented her with a bill for costs, which exceeded the total backpayments of maintenance he had succeeded in obtaining; fortunately, with Baba's help that bill was challenged and substantially reduced. The mortgage payments having, inevitably, also fallen into arrears, another attorney failed to inform Maria that the insurance company for which Roger worked, and with whom Roger had negotiated the mortgage, had foreclosed on the farm; this was a development of which Maria heard by chance from neighbors.

When it was discovered in the relevant documentation that only twenty acres of the sixty-acre property had been mortgaged, the insurance company reacted by claiming that there had been a so-called scrivener's error, and applied to the court for an amendment to include the whole property. Roger, still associated with the company, testified that both he and Maria had always intended to mortgage the whole property; Maria contested this, but had to admit that during the marriage she had usually signed whatever Roger had asked her to sign. So it went on, an unbroken chain of obstruction and calamities. Maria would be the first to say that without Baba's help she could never have navigated a way through the mesh of difficulties she encountered. It was an object lesson for all about the impossibility for a woman on her own and without independent resources to obtain justice in such circumstances, faced with power structures intent on disempowering her.

Renée constantly stood by Maria and helped her at every stage, using almost every leave day available to her to drive with Maria to her local courthouse, and attending all the court hearings and related meetings. As usual, whenever I was in the States, I too participated, attending meetings and hearings and spending many hours preparing letters on behalf of Maria to the state attorney general and others about various aspects of her case.

In the end the aforementioned leading Minnesota real estate attorney came into the picture again with his calm and wise advice. He said that the best outcome would be to *lose* the case about the scrivener's error, since there would then be an interval while new documentation was prepared during which there would be no current mortgage and no foreclosure. If Baba could help Maria to sell the property during that interval, Maria could pay off the remaining sum and arrears from the old mortgage and all back taxes and other outstanding debts, and would be in the clear at last. That was precisely what happened but it took Baba's U.S.-wide contacts and his exceptional business acumen to achieve it. As already mentioned, the entire process required eight and a half years to run its course.

Maria had studied Art at college and in later years developed a marked talent for photography. Another young Minnesotan, Nancy Bundt, a student and friend of Audrey Flack, had with Baba's early help and encouragement taken up photography as a career and become an internationally successful professional photographer. During the 1970s and '80s Nancy took thousands of photographs of Baba and his friends and activities, in both the United States and India. Later, she married a Norwegian and moved to Norway, but whenever she visited Minnesota she continued to do remarkable photographic work for Baba.

Subsequently, Maria made at least two hundred videos of and about Baba. She also restored and preserved many priceless, old photographs, which were otherwise in danger of succumbing to the tropical dampness of the Kerala monsoons. Maria's video records of Baba's roses, lilies and other flowers are works of art in themselves, as is her fine video study of Baba's Shrine of Silence at Prasanth. A video she made in 2002 of Baba's return with Savithri and others to a small Shankaracharya temple high in the Kodashadri hills in the State of Karnataka, to which Baba had climbed in 1952 soon after he had left home on his quest for his spiritual Master, was so outstanding that a film producer who saw it said he would gladly have employed her as a photographer for one of his films.

Until the end of Baba's life, Maria also filled a real need by helping Baba in the home while others were out at work, acting as his driver and, especially, helping him to create his beautiful gardens. She also helped Baba with, and shared, his love of working with wood. After Baba left his body, Maria opted to start a new life on her own; however, her legacy of photographic work stands as an outstanding contribution for the future and as evidence of her gratitude and her great love for Baba.

CHAPTER FIFTEEN

"Beloved Baba gave the only gift worthy of being received in silence. The gift of love. He said, "Spread it like fire."

He set me aflame. This flame consumes everything, leaving nothing behind. If one is blessed to be aflame with love one allows himself to be consumed in silence. Words can never express what this means"

Baba in Silence, February 1962

All the legal fights and skirmishes so far described ended well for us. There was, however, one case, brought against Baba himself, that he would not and did not turn to his advantage.

In November 1993, Baba came from the United States at short notice to spend two or three weeks with me in our home in Marple, near Stockport in the northwest of England. He told me one day in passing that before going on to India to spend some time with his ninety-two-year-old mother he planned to help "one woman" in England. When a woman living in Manchester told us that her nineteen-year-old daughter was causing her anxiety, Baba was, as always, prepared to do what he could to help. The mother told us that the daughter had had a motor accident that had affected her badly; she had been seen by three neurologists but no one could find what was wrong with her. Now she had lost her job and become aimless, getting up very late and spending hours every day in the shower. We invited mother and daughter to our house for a dinner on the following Sunday.

Baba himself prepared a delicious meal for our guests, and on the Sunday evening, the mother and daughter arrived for dinner, unexpectedly accompanied by the mother's male friend. During dinner, Baba explained that he was not a medical doctor but had experience of helping people with similar problems; he would be happy to do what he could for the young woman if they would feel confident to leave her with him for a couple of days, while I would be at work. We had an engagement on the evening of the third day, so by then she would have to be back at home.

After some private discussion with her mother and the mother's friend, the young woman told us she wanted to come but must bring her two small dogs with her, which we said was no problem. Late that night, we took her in our car, following the mother and friend in their car, some twenty miles across Manchester to pick up a few things the daughter would need, plus the dogs and their paraphernalia, and then she and her dogs drove back with us. She was given a room for herself and her dogs and we all went to bed.

Next morning, after we had foregathered in Baba's room for tea, I left for work as expected

Early in the afternoon, I was summoned home by a neighbor. When I arrived, Baba told me that the young woman had asked if she could take her dogs for a walk and had not returned. Thinking she might have lost her way, I drove with Baba all around the neighborhood looking for her. Eventually, I rang the mother to say we were worried because her daughter had disappeared. The mother's response was surprisingly calm and no doubt that was when I should have understood that something was up. Meanwhile, there was nothing more we could do.

Late that evening, there was a knock at the door and standing on our doorstep were two uniformed policemen and a policewoman. They told me the young woman had formally complained to them that she had been improperly treated at our house.

At the Committal hearing before Stockport magistrates, when they would decide whether the case was suitable to be dealt with by them, the defense has no right to speak. The woman acting for the prosecution gave a brief account of what was alleged, in which it was stated, quite wrongly, that the young woman had been required to sleep with Baba. With the benefit of hindsight, perhaps I should have identified myself to the court as a fellow magistrate—not in Stockport but in Manchester City—and said that what the magistrates had just heard was seriously misleading. Unfortunately, I obeyed the rules. With that distorted version of the allegation, the case was sent to be heard after many months by a Manchester judge and jury, instead of being dealt with in a few weeks by local magistrates.

On being assured that Baba had handed over his passport and would be staying with me, the Stockport magistrates granted bail and with profound relief we were free to go home. The policeman who handed Baba his belongings as he left the courthouse inadvertently also returned to him his passport! We kept it with our lawyer but Baba could have left England and gone to be with his mother at any time during the fourteen months it took for the case to be heard. I am sure he never considered doing so.

So in due course, an almost all-white Manchester jury came to choose between a foreign visitor who did not speak and whose written evidence was read out by his lawyer, and a young white woman of their city. The only piece of independent evidence before them had come from the taxi driver who took the young woman home;

she described her as normal and chatty. There was no allegation of sex, of hurt, nor any other objective evidence. Despite all the other published and spoken evidence before them of Baba's character and record, by a majority they found Baba guilty as charged.

No words can describe my feelings on seeing Baba, calm and silent in the court, being convicted and, later, sentenced. Could those who so judged Baba—or most people, really—even begin to imagine, if nothing else, what it takes to keep silence for (till then) thirty-three years, while living a full and active life in the world? Soon afterwards, I resigned as a magistrate, sold my home and, being by then just retired, went to be from then on with Baba in the United States or India.

When this whole episode had run its course, Baba simply resumed his life as before. He had been fully aware of what was happening at every point, including in the jury-room. Those of us who had been close to Baba for decades, not hours, knew that in all circumstances he would be helping people, not harming them. We also knew that anything that happened with Baba always had some larger purpose. Nevertheless, for us there was bitter sorrow in what such a man had to endure.

Strangeways in Manchester, England

The law, once activated, will always lumber on its way and Beloved Baba, who as a young man had at the behest of his spiritual Master lived in total seclusion for a year on only two cups of tea and one orange a day, now spent almost three months sharing the life of prisoners in the jail in Manchester. Being silent, he could only communicate with them by writing, but what he found most trying was the noise from the prison officers' shouting. Baba never touched the prison food; he subsisted instead on dried fruit and nuts from the shop and one glass of fresh milk daily. The milk was secured for him by the governor of his wing, who before long was visiting Baba almost every day.

Baba told us privately about several incidents, one of which I share as follows. It seems that new arrivals, apart from regulars, were given some quiet time in a sick bay to begin to come to terms with what had happened to them. Baba was silently sitting there soon after his arrival when a fellow inmate came and stood nearby, looking at him intently. This had begun to be a little disconcerting when the man suddenly approached Baba and asked him to take off his shoes. Baba did so. Then the man asked him to take off his socks. Baba did that too. Then this man bent down and kissed Baba's feet.

He told Baba he was a member of the Irish Republican Army—to himself a freedom fighter, to the British government a criminal because of certain acts committed by him against the British Army in Northern Ireland. Whatever the facts of his case, after a few minutes of close observation this man had seen something about Baba that had eluded those who had put Baba where he was. There need be no doubt that wherever Baba was, in whatever circumstances, his presence would be a blessing to those who encountered him, whether, as in this instance, it was recognized, or not.

Another Young Woman—Renata

During the many months that Baba waited in England for his day in court another young woman, Renata, became close to him. Renata's story enables me to draw this account to a conclusion on a happier note.

Renata was brought up in Czechoslovakia before the break-up of the Soviet bloc. As a girl, she was very independent, not to say rebellious, having no interest in studying beyond the end of her school days. In her teens she found what employment she could and, after the Velvet Revolution in 1989, when the communist regime was brought to an end, she started to work as an interpreter for an American woman who was reintroducing to Czech people the ancient healing art of Reiki. With this woman's help, Renata came to England and in due course met Baba. Renata recognized Baba at once as someone she used to see in a dream.

Having been raised under communism, Renata began by telling Baba she was an atheist—she hoped he would not mind? Of course he would not mind! It probably does not matter all that much what we sometimes think we think; what matters more is our heart's capacity to love. Renata, who was by then living with a family in London, started coming to our house in Marple whenever she could to be with Baba and Baba persuaded her to resume her studies.

With the full support of the family with whom she was living, Renata quickly gained her BSc degree in Psychology from the University of Surrey. She and the family wanted her to stay with them and study for a master's degree, which they would have been happy to finance. However, the Czech Republic was not yet part of the European Union and the British immigration authorities would not renew her visa so she had to leave England. Renata worked for a while as an educational psychologist at a school in the Czech Republic, taking six weeks' leave of absence as soon as she could to travel to India and visit Baba and Savithri in Prasanth.

Soon afterwards, Baba arranged with the help of two Czech professors, one a long-time friend of Renée and her family and the other the honorary Czech consul in Minneapolis, for Renata to be enrolled on a scholarship as a graduate student in the Special Education department at the University of Minnesota. With Baba's continuing help and support, Renata gained first her Master's degree and then her Doctorate in Special Education; her supervisors rated her ability so highly that she was given a full-time research post in the department even before she completed her dissertation. Thereafter, Renata made rapid progress in her chosen field, winning grants for her team, addressing conferences and working with Special Education colleagues in other countries as well as the United States.

Renata dedicated her life to Baba and lived with Baba as a member of the family in New Brighton throughout the course of her studies and subsequently. It was a pleasure to see Baba's satisfaction in her achievements and his enjoyment of her company. In October 2009 Renata, accompanied by Baba, visited her home in the Czech Republic for the first time in nine years, and was able to introduce Baba to her parents and family.

End and Beginning

Baba dropped his body, as it is said in India of someone of his spiritual standing, in Minneapolis at 5:17 a.m. on March 27, 2010. The body was taken to India to be buried on the hill above Baba's Shrine of Silence in Prasanth. Baba's tomb is very simply and beautifully made of pure white marble and the design for the large temple structure over it reflects a characteristically Keralite style of sacred building.

Julia, a seven-year-old child, daughter of friends living nearby in New Brighton, quietly observed to her mother as they were leaving our house after visiting soon after Baba had left his body: "I miss Baba, but now he can do his work even better." I do not think I could find a more fitting way to end this brief memoir than with words of such rare understanding from the mouth of a child.

Baba's self-portrait in oils, Simla, c. 1965. Kept in Prasanth.

Audrey Flack: *"Baba"*, 1980-83, acrylic and oil on canvas, 7.5' x 13'. Reproduced courtesy of the artist and the Butler Institute of American Art, Youngstown, Ohio, USA.

Portrait of Baba by Elizabeth Brunner, New
Delhi, 1960 (before Silence).

'Baba: "Don't paint me with a halo, Lizzie!"
Lizzie: "Baba, I paint what I see."

Portrait of Baba, *"The Enlightened One"*, terracotta,
by Elizabeth Brunner, New Delhi, 1971.

Baba at the Grand Canyon, Arizona, USA.

Savithri, in Prasanth.

Savithri at Bekal Fort in North Kerala, beside the Arabian Sea

Renée enjoying "Grace", a gift hand-made
for Baba by a friend, Ilonka Harezi.

Renata—Graduation Day.
*(Note also the picture behind Renata of Audrey Flack
standing near her painting of Baba, which shows its
scale. The other pictures are of Meher Baba.)*

APPENDIX 1

The following is the last talk Mouni Baba gave, before a distinguished audience in the Bharathiya Vidya Bhavan, Rafi Marg, New Delhi on February 24, 1962. At 5.00 a.m. the following day, Meher Baba's birthday, Baba at the age of 32 entered his life-long Silence in the presence of a smaller, invited group in Maharajah Rajendra Singh of Shivpuri's palace in Friends Colony, New Delhi.

SILENCE

The Presence of Beloved Baba is so full of silence that one expects The Word to emerge at any moment but what comes is only a greater silence. It is through silence the first meeting between man and the Mystery of God is accomplished. God's Silence is Real. In silence He receives the love of His lovers and in silence He loves those who deny Him.

Mysterious is the silence of mystics. Mystic revelation is only possible when silence is perfected. In them silence is an expression of the blessedness of the inner freedom. In silence they listen to God's blissful song of His sacred Word. God has been eternally singing in silence, unobserved, unheard except by those who experience His infinite Silence. Above the tumult of voices His Silence reigns supreme. In silence, it is possible for man to surrender completely to God; then God reveals Himself in His full glory, His infinite power, His unfathomable knowledge and His eternal existence.

Silence—it is pure existence. In the absolute sense, silence has neither a beginning nor end. It abides as the only Reality. It is ever the uncreated, everlasting Being in existence. Even though silence is an all-pervading Reality, there are hardly a few who experience it. This experience is different from every other kind of experience. To experience silence is to get lost in silence. One has to lose everything including oneself if God is to be found. All the words spoken from the beginningless beginning to the endless end also get lost in the Infinite Silence of God. Blessed is the Word that comes forth from the fullness of silence. God created this universe with that sacred Word. Only in silence the Word of God can be heard. By merely avoiding speech one is far from being silent. When silence ceases to be the guiding force, however, the apparent quietness might be idleness. If one allows himself to be consumed by idleness, life becomes tragic. Silence is not inaction. It transcends both action and inaction.

Have you ever imagined a world where there is nothing but silence? In the world of silence, eternity IS. Pure time exists in silence as timelessness. Silence is a basic phenomenon which cannot be traced back to anything else. In silence man can witness the original being of all things. In silence the limitless and the limited are all together. Silence can exist without speech but speech cannot exist without silence. When the tree of life is manured with silence the blossoms of happiness and contentment are at their best. All the misery and unhappiness in man is because the silence in man has exploded. When I look at the present-day human life it appears to be the ruins of silence.

Words of men are not authority. In the absolute sense all words are too inflexible, because at the most they can only suggest the Real. So long as a path of attainment exists, words may be useful; one may receive inspiration from the words of great ones. It is philosophically more easy to teach the entire world than to point out the path for one sincere aspirant. Simple speech conveys most truth. Extensive logic, diction and commentaries are putrid – ignorance shielding itself. The true ones tread the mystic path in all humility, guided by the Perfect One in Silence. When man realizes the Eternal, his karma is finished and goal attained. The goal being achieved, NOW remains the only possible consciousness. In living NOW there can be no goal.

In renunciation of search lies peace, but this cannot be forced by mental discipline or external aids. Renunciation comes when you are ready. Fleeing from one's family is no solution. Those who flee are never free. Freedom faces creation, bondage seeks to escape environment. Stop, when silence knocks. Let go, and know at last thine own. Letting go is never to a known object. If you have mastered control of senses, stop controlling and renounce to the Whole. Then such an ecstatic force that a thousand religious reformers could not produce will enter and transmute your being. Then you will know the purpose of your devotion and wisdom of mastery. You will know the first and the last. But above all, you will KNOW. To be all absorbed in cosmic consciousness is to be unconscious of individuality. In individuality lies distortion. One understands this when his silence is perfected. Present, past, future dissolve into Silence Eternal.

In silence, if you could be conscious of your ignorance, your attitude is reverent. Conscious ignorance is humility. Divine ignorance is human. Human ignorance is divine. Perfect silence is illumination. Illumination expresses itself in golden waves of silence. In illumination one transcends thoughts; thoughts are but shadows of the consciousness that projects them into this form. There are many who give sermons and discourses about the mystery of God. It often fails to affect humanity deeply, because those words fail to come out of silence. God cannot be discussed or argued about. God is to be realized in silence. Man in his ignorance sometimes feels that noise has overpowered silence. Man becomes restless when the silence in him goes to sleep. Deep silence gives man the power to make his noisy years seem moments in the being of the Eternal Silence. In deep silence God ceases to be an object but becomes an experience. In the world of noise life is governed by the possibility of illusions.

Blessed is the silence of nature. It awakens in man an intuitive feeling of the great Silence that was before the Word and out of which everything arose. Through silence one could be connected to everything in nature. Silence is present in every man as the only Reality. Only when silence is awakened, all that is unreal goes to everlasting sleep. The miracle of silence is that where death might be—the Beloved appears.

When the canoe of words glides down the river of silence, music emanates. Silence in music has always charmed me. Music at its best is always the pause, the rest, the moment of silence. The state or condition when nothing is audible – absence of all sound or noise. Complete quietness or stillness, noiselessness sometimes personified. Silence is never more audible than when the last sound of music has died away.

Beloved Baba gave the only gift worthy of being received in silence, the Gift of Love. He said, "Spread it like fire." He set me aflame. This flame consumes everything, leaving nothing behind. If one is blessed to be aflame with love one allows himself to be consumed in silence. Words can never express what this means.

Blessed is silence. In silence you can rise from thought to the fullness of Pure Knowing and rest in your own true being.

APPENDIX 2

The following is the full text of Baba's message read out at Dadaji's Ramnavami meeting (see page 105).

My life is like a dewdrop on a perfect bloom

It is the teardrop shed by the Angel of Silence.

To adorn beauty, I borrow a ray of light

And behold the Eternal Mystery for a moment.

The Enlightened One transcends knowledge.

He is one with the Eternal Light that pervades the cosmos.

This light is ever the same everywhere.

Blessed is he who can see the Divine Light with the Divine Eye.

Only when all that is unreal goes to everlasting sleep

Are you awakened by God's grace to see the hidden light

That shines everywhere.

Be sure of my silent help.

BABA

APPENDIX 3

Here, to end with, is an example of something written by Baba:

Blind Old Man
He sees everything
No-one sees Him

Deaf Old Man
He hears everything
No-one hears Him

Dumb Old Man
He speaks with no tongue
In all the tongues
No-one listens

Old Old Man
No-one to touch Him
He touches everyone

Old Old Man
He can't even smell
Yet spreads fragrance

Old Old Man
You are treasured
In Him

All Love
BABA

About the Author

After retiring with an MBE as Director of Social Policy at the British Equal Opportunities Commission in 1995, Brenda Hancock has divided her years almost entirely between Baba's homes in New Brighton, Minnesota and North Kerala, India.

Lightning Source UK Ltd.
Milton Keynes UK
UKHW05f2251150518
322635UK00007B/97/P